What Readers Are Sayi
Modern Management Mad

"The lessons I learned reading *Modern Manage.* books make me a better leader. Descriptive examples paint a c.. picture of situations at work I often find myself in, and applying the practical advice helps me better serve myself, my team, and my organization. Johanna influenced me to think congruently, and provided the tools needed to excel in my role. I can't recommend these books highly enough."

— CARL HUME, VP ENGINEERING AT HOMESTARS

"If you are starting a new management role, or simply want a reminder of what it is all about, then these books provide a body of practical wisdom in an easily digestible form. They place the role of the manager in a wider context rather that implying some context free set of qualities and manage to avoid the platitudes all too common in books of this kind."

—DAVE SNOWDEN, CHIEF SCIENTIFIC OFFICER, COGNITIVE EDGE

"Do you need real-world answers to real-world management problems, especially to address agility at all levels? As I read Johanna Rothman's *Modern Management Made Easy* books, I nodded along and said, "I've seen that!" Use these books with their suggestions for what you can do to solve your real-world management problems."

— SCOTT SEIVWRIGHT, AGILE COACH AND LEADERSHIP PIRATE

"This series of books is a rare mix of personal stories, practical examples, researched theory, and direct calls-to-action. Rarer still, Johanna's writing segues between them without losing the reader or breaking their immersion. Whether you are a manager, an aspiring manager, or a coach of managers, these books will give you the necessary tools to develop new skills and the language to develop new cultures."

— EVAN LEYBOURN, CO-FOUNDER, BUSINESS AGILITY INSTITUTE

"Think of these books like three friends who can offer you advice on your management journey. You'll return to them whenever you want advice, reassurance, challenge, or renewal. I added these books to my library, right next to the late Russell Ackoff's books on the F/laws of management. Use these books to create your modern management and an environment that brings out the best in the people you lead and serve."

—CLAUDE EMOND, ORGANIZATIONAL PERFORMANCE-GROWTH EXPERT

"This book series is the furthest thing from your run-of-the-mill boring management books. Johanna Rothman busts dozens of management myths in an easy to read set of essays that are useful in part or as a whole. The stories and anecdotes told are relatable, practical, and fit for today's modern workplace. Regardless of your management experience, there's valuable lessons to be found on every single page."

—RYAN DORRELL, CO-FOUNDER, AGILETHOUGHT

"These books provide a wealth of practical leadership and team-building information. Project managers and leaders of problem-solving teams are often taught logical but flawed guidance from the industrial era. Today's project teams require servant leadership, inspiration, and collaboration skills far more than centralized planning or progress tracking. Johanna's books identify and bring to life better alternatives for undertaking challenging projects. Laid out in a helpful sequence, they provide a wealth of practical tools for today's practitioner searching for better outcomes and more satisfied stakeholders."

—MIKE GRIFFITHS, CEO, LEADING ANSWERS INC.

"If you lead at any level in today's disrupted and crazy world, read these books on modern management. As with all Johanna's books, they are full of insightful stories, real world examples and concrete actionable advice. Use these books to guide your own development, support and lead others, and guide your organisation to greater success."

—SHANE HASTIE, DIRECTOR OF COMMUNITY DEVELOPMENT ICAGILE

"Each product team has its own culture. It is important for leaders to understand where culture comes from and how they can influence it so that their teams can build better products. In the *Modern Management Made Easy* books, Johanna Rothman has some valuable advice to help you be more purposefully create a culture that will support the team while driving powerful innovations. Her style of writing includes questioning and addressing industry myths that draw from decades of real world experience. Her work will change the way you lead product."

—SEAN FLAHERTY, EVP OF INNOVATION AND COHOST OF THE PRODUCT MOMENTUM PODCAST.

"With her characteristic blend of pragmatism, insight, and wit, Johanna Rothman takes on the role of modern management's mirror, mythbuster, and mentor. The first in her *Modern Management Made Easy* trilogy, *Practical Ways to Manage Yourself* demystifies the illusions we knowledge workers spin. Offering thought-provoking observations from her own career, along with steps to help identify and replace outmoded thinking and habits while gently urging guiding the reader towards a more thoughtful management practice, this latest volume reinforces why Johanna remains among modern management's most readable, relevant, and respected thinkers."

—TONIANNE DEMARIA, COAUTHOR OF SHINGO-AWARD WINNING *Personal Kanban*

Practical Ways to
Lead and Serve (Manage) Others

Modern Management Made Easy: Book 2

Johanna Rothman

Practical Ink

Arlington, Massachusetts

Practical Ways to Lead and Serve (Manage) Others
Modern Management Made Easy: Book 2

Johanna Rothman

Published by Practical Ink
www.jrothman.com

Practical **ink**

Cover design: Brandon Swann, swanndesignstudio.com
Cover art: Company Value Icons by Angela Cini, on depositphotos.com

Ebook: 978-1-943487-15-8
Print: 978-1-943487-16-5
Hardcover: 978-1-943487-17-2

In memory and honor of Jerry Weinberg who told me I should write a book about rewiring management logic.

For Edward Rothman, my first management mentor.

And, for Mark, Shaina and Adam, and Naomi and Matt, as always. Thank you for managing me.

Contents

CHAPTER 3

How Often Do You Meet Privately With People? 29

CHAPTER 4

Do I Really Need to Tell Someone How They're Doing? . . 41

List of Figures

Acknowledgments

I thank all the people who read and commented on the management myths columns as I wrote them. I also thank Software Quality Engineering, now known as Techwell, who first published these columns.

I thank my coaching and consulting clients. You have taught me more than you know.

I thank Matt Barcomb, Pawel Brodzinski, Lisa Crispin, Andrea Goulet, Mike Lowery, Carl Hume, and Leland Newsom for their technical review.

I thank Rebecca Airmet and Nancy Groth for their editing. I thank Brandon Swann for his cover design. I thank Karen Billipp for her layout and Jean Jesensky for her indexing.

Any mistakes are mine.

Introduction

Several years ago, I wrote a series of articles I called "management myths." They each described one way I'd seen managers act so that the manager created the opposite result from the one they wanted. Yes, the manager's actions created precisely the opposite effect.

I wrote a myth a month for 36 months.

I assumed as the world transitioned to agile approaches or approaches where teams, managers, and organizations needed more resilience, that managers would change. I thought no one needed to read about the myths in a world where we want collaborative, cross-functional, self-managing teams.

I was wrong.

As I worked with more managers who wanted to use agile approaches, I saw several problems with their management practices:

- The practices barely worked for non-agile teams. Teams succeeded in spite of their management.
- The practices prevented any team's adaptability and resilience.
- The practices didn't work for managers who wanted to lead and serve others.

And, in an organization attempting to transform to an agile culture? The more the managers tried to make old patterns work, the less agility anyone exhibited.

Why did these smart people behave in ways that didn't make sense?

They didn't know any better.

These managers had never witnessed useful management, never mind excellent management. They tried to do the best job they could. And, they perpetuated what they'd experienced, or possibly even learned in school. They practiced what they'd seen—the old ways of management.

It's time for real modern management.

Modern managers face enormous challenges. Too many managers feel as if they are stuck between the proverbial rock and a hard place.

How can you become a modern manager when the system, the culture, is based on old thinking and old practices?

Carefully.

I've divided the original essays into three books. Book 1, *Practical Ways to Manage Yourself,* asks you to consider how you can manage and respect yourself to build congruence and integrity in your actions.

This second book explains how you can serve a harmonic whole. The entire team or group can then work together in a culture of transparency and trust.

Book 3, *Practical Ways to Lead an Innovative Organization,* explores ways to create a human and innovative culture in your organization, so you can use the ideas of trust and integrity to create a place where people want to work.

You might feel many constraints in your situation. As you read these books, you might nod and say, "Yes, I can do that." And, you might shake your head at some ideas and say, "Not going to touch that here. Nope, not at all."

I do hope you consider each essay as a possible experiment for your management practice. You have options.

Who Are the People in These Essays?

You might wonder about my use of names and gender in these books. For example, you might never have seen women as senior managers. I have seen men and women as senior managers. I've been a senior manager.

My experience tells me that a given gender does not equate to great or unfortunate management skills. Neither does a person's country of origin or any other kind of individual demographic.

To help you see what the management world could be, I've created parity across genders. I've used names of people I've worked with or admired. Even with that, I've changed all the names to protect the innocent and the guilty.

I've had the good fortune to meet and work with male and female managers worldwide. In almost every circumstance, the managers have done the best they could, given their company's environment and culture. The manager's gender didn't matter.

The company's environment mattered more than anything. You might—or might not—see the variety of people in roles that I write about here.

Through my work, I've recognized several principles that create great management and build healthy organizational cultures.

1. Clarify purpose—for you, the team, and the organization.
2. Build empathy with the people who do the work.
3. Build a safe environment. People work better when they can trust you, their colleagues, and the organization as a whole.
4. Seek outcomes by optimizing for an overarching goal.
5. Encourage experiments and learning.

6. Catch people succeeding.
7. Exercise value-based integrity as a model for the people you lead and serve.

All three books build on these principles:

- Respect—for yourself, for the team, and for the purpose of the organization.
- Trust—possibly with boundaries—to encourage the behaviors and outcomes you want.
- Team-based approaches to working at all levels of the organization.

All three books explain some of the trickier parts of management. You'll get the most value if you read all three books.

As you read the dialogue in the essays, remember that I said most of these things to my managers. You might see these conversations as insubordination.

I didn't feel as if I was insubordinate. I used the principle of congruence to have conversations where my manager and I cared about the outcome, each other, and discovered our best possible outcome for the situation.

You and I are different people. How I frame conversations might not work for you. You will find *your* best ways to describe the situation and influence your manager.

You can practice human and humane management that produces superior results for your organization. You can respect yourself, the people you serve, and the entire organization and customers. You can act with integrity. And, you can have empathy without being a pushover.

Management is an honorable profession. We need managers—great, congruent managers who can use their interpersonal skills to get the best out of themselves first. Then, they can extend those skills to the people they serve and across the organization.

My best to you. I hope you enjoy reading these essays and that you act to ease your way into modern management.

Let's start.

CHAPTER 1

Managers Lead and Serve Others

When I work with managers, I ask them what they want from the people they lead. They say things like this:

- I want to know I can trust the people to do a great job and deliver great work.
- I want to know that the people are engaged and working hard to serve our customers.
- I want to know that the people are loyal to their team and the purpose of the organization.

How many of your management practices encourage these behaviors?

Here's what I see too often:

- People feel as if they can't do a great job—they don't have the time they need or the people they need to deliver their best work.
- People feel as if they are interchangeable cogs. The work doesn't engage or challenge them. They might not even know the purpose of this work.
- People don't feel loyalty to their team or the organization.

And the managers? They feel more and more pressure to deliver results. The managers often resort to directing and controlling the people they manage to achieve those results.

Consider this reframe: instead of managing other people, great managers lead and serve others.

When managers lead and serve, they can trust people. The people engage themselves and deliver the requested results. The managers create an environment where people engage themselves and develop loyalty to their teams, products, and the organization.

How do these great managers lead and serve? Peter Drucker, in *Management: Tasks, Responsibilities, Practices* [DRU73], wrote that managers exist to fulfill these two specific tasks:

1. Create a team or workgroup that exists as a harmonic whole—the whole team or group is greater than the sum of its parts.
2. Balance the immediate and long-term future.

Managers lead when they create a team that can solve problems where those problems exist.

Managers who create a harmonic whole lead and serve. And, using that harmonic whole, they can balance the immediate and long-term futures. The manager can create an environment where people can do their best work.

We have a name for a harmonic whole: flow efficiency.

1.2 Encourage Flow Efficiency

Current management practices perpetuate a big misunderstanding about how people work effectively in the organization. Too often, we treat people as individuals, as resources. That misunderstanding has a name—resource efficiency.

Each person has their specific expertise. When the person on the left completes their work, they hand off that work to the person on the

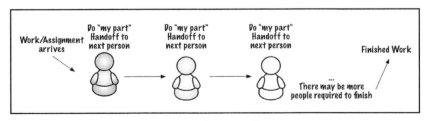

Figure 1.1: Resource Efficiency

right, the person next in line. That person finishes his or her work and passes the work on to the next person on the right. And, if the people discover a problem, the work often returns to the front of the line, the left-most person. Every handoff requires waiting until the person is ready for the work.

Resource efficiency looks efficient, right? Resource efficiency says If we divide and conquer the work, we can do it faster.

For knowledge work, that's wrong.

When we hand off work to each other, instead of working as a harmonious team, we increase the delays in the team. All the work takes much longer than if we worked together.

When managers use resource efficiency, each person is a specialist. That means a specific expert—and only that expert—can do their work. You might have seen this cycle: the expert becomes more expert and specialized. Pretty soon, that expert is the only one in the organization who can do the work, and it takes too long to bring other people in to even learn about the work.

With resource efficiency, you optimize for each person along the way. You get the finished work when you get it.

Resource efficiency focuses on output. Each person does their job. However, outputs don't necessarily create valuable outcomes—a product or service a customer can use.

In resource efficiency, each person is "fully utilized." That full utilization leads to problems such as:

- "It takes forever to bring people up to speed around here."
- "Only Fred can work on that. He's the only one who knows that code (or whatever)."
- "You can't take a vacation. That's just before we want to ship, and you're the only one who knows that part of the product."
- Many features are partly done, and too few are complete. (The work in progress is quite high.)

It's very safe for managers to think in resource-efficiency terms. When we do, we can "hold people accountable," we can attempt to measure each person's contribution and rank the people, and we can blame people for "not doing their jobs."

Contrast that with flow efficiency, the idea in *This is Lean: Resolving the Efficiency Paradox* [MOA13].

Figure 1.2: Flow Efficiency

When we use flow efficiency, the *team* takes the item and collaborates. The team might specialize in a particular area of the product, but the entire team collaborates to finish a given piece of work.

What happens if someone is out for a day or a week? The team can complete the work without that person. Yes, the team might be a little slower, but they can still release finished work.

When teams work in flow efficiency, it doesn't matter what each person "knows." The team optimizes its collaboration to finish the work. Teams take these kinds of actions:

- The team limits the total work they undertake for a given amount of time.
- The team decides how they collaborate. They might pair, swarm, or mob to finish their work.
- The team might use limits to manage their WIP (Work in Progress), regardless of the state of the work.

Resource efficiency is about optimizing at the level of the individual, for outputs. Flow efficiency is about optimizing for the team's throughput, for outcomes.

Customers can't buy busy-ness. Customers can only buy completed and shippable work.

Flow efficiency helps teams finish work faster. Resource efficiency creates delays.

Modern managers encourage flow efficiency. They don't manage for resource efficiency.

Flow efficiency requires that managers change their behaviors first, and then their mindset. These changes are tricky. That's because the words we use in organizations reinforce resource-efficiency thinking:

- We call the people who help with employee hiring, retention, and engagement "Human Resources."
- "Resources" work on projects.
- Some people do "load balancing" for humans working on several projects at a time.

If you use flow efficiency, you are more likely to get the results you want. That means you can trust everyone to do their jobs—and trust that the team can deliver the results you want. Trust is the next big idea for leading and serving others.

Flow Efficiency for Workgroups

If you manage a workgroup as opposed to an interdependent team, you might be puzzled. How can you use the ideas of flow efficiency where people are supposed to work alone?

Here's how one Customer Support group used flow efficiency thinking:

- Every time they hired a new person, they had the new person pair with one buddy for a couple of weeks.

- Every time people rotated to a new area of expertise, the new person paired with an experienced person in that new area.

> - If anyone realized after 15 minutes they were stuck, they hung a ticket on a kanban board and continued to work on the issue. As each person finished their tickets, they would first check the board to see if anyone needed help.
>
> No one felt alone. No one felt as if they were stuck. That workgroup worked as a team when they could, and individuals when they didn't need to.

When we, as managers, manage for collaboration, we change the culture. That collaboration allows everyone to function as the best person they can be.

A harmonic whole requires more than a reasonable flow of work. Harmony also requires psychological safety.

1.2 Create a Culture of Psychological Safety

Psychological safety starts with how safe you feel to discuss issues, and experiment.

You might think it matters how safe the people you serve feel—and that's a big piece of managing others. However, if you don't feel safe as a manager, you can't extend that safety to the people you serve.

Amy C. Edmondson, in *Teaming: How Organizations Learn, Innovate, and Compete in the Knowledge Economy* [EDM12], discusses the need for psychological safety in interdependent collaborative teams.

Edmondson's five points about safety are:

- Use clear and direct language.
- Encourage learning from small experiments.
- Admit when we don't know.
- Acknowledge when we fail.
- Set boundaries for what is a personal or team decision and what is not.

Safety allows the team members to discuss, explore together, and learn. You are also part of at least one interdependent collaborative team—the management team at your level. If you and your peers don't feel safe to ask for help, to create experiments, and set reasonable boundaries, the people you serve won't feel safe either.

That safety—or lack thereof—permeates the entire organization even if you don't have a highly interdependent team. Here's an example that includes how your organization rewards people:

- If the organization punishes people for making mistakes, why would anyone take a chance?
- If the organization punishes people for collaboration, why would anyone collaborate?
- If the organization punishes people for thinking quietly, why would anyone want to appear less than fully busy?

That lack of safety drags the entire organization down. That's one of the reasons people think management can exist without leadership. The leaders stick their necks out and ask for help, admit when they're wrong, and experiment.

If you don't feel safe to ask for help, the people you serve can't ask for what they want. You'll have plenty of paperwork-based management. You'll cover your tush. Everyone else will cover theirs.

And, too few people will want to experiment. You won't be able to lead or serve.

Many of the essays in this book are about your safety so you can lead and serve others.

Edmonson offers a tool for fostering psychological safety.[1]

One way I like to think about how safety affects how we treat each other is in how we extend or don't extend trust.

[1] https://rework.withgoogle.com/guides/understanding-team-effectiveness/steps/foster-psychological-safety/

1.3 **Extend Trust**

Are you supposed to trust the people you serve to do their jobs? Many organizations ask for status details that require a manager to micromanage—not serve—people. (I wrote about this in Book 1.)

Consider how you manage your life. You probably have a mortgage or pay rent every month. That means you manage your money.

You get yourself to work on time, fed, and clothed. You manage your personal needs.

You might have more responsibilities, such as with or to a spouse, family, pets. Maybe even to other organizations outside your family, such as your town or places you volunteer. You manage your responsibilities to others.

You are an adult who recognizes and manages your responsibilities. Things might happen that prevent you from delivering all the time—and you let people know when that occurs. Other people trust you.

You're an adult. So are the people you serve. You can extend trust to them, too.

A quick check: how many policies and procedures do you have, that you, as a manager, need to follow? (I'm not talking about physical safety policies, such as closed-toe shoes or safety glasses in labs. I'm talking about other policies such as around work hours, what people can spend money on, and how you think about hiring.) The more policies and procedures, the less trust you extend.

Adults don't need a lot of direction or control. They need to understand the reasons for the work you requested, the boundaries of their decision-making, the ability to integrate learning into their work, and the strength to work with others. You and they might need to agree on when to check in with each other, but you don't have to micromanage their work.

Consider these trust-building actions, as in Solomon in *Building Trust in Business, Politics, Relationships, and Life* [SOF01]:

- Deliver what you promise to deliver.

- Be consistent in your actions and reactions.
- Make integrity a cornerstone of your work.
- Be willing to discuss, influence, and negotiate. Don't get stuck on your position.
- Trust in yourself and your colleagues.

When you trust people and serve them, you might:

- Decide what to measure that makes sense for the system and the person. Then, you might offer feedback when things do or don't go the way you want.
- Create an environment in which people can do their best work. How can you create an environment of ease? How can you avoid creating challenges that make the work more difficult?
- Create an environment in which people feel that both their team and manager support their work.

You might think of trust and safety as a balancing act—part of your management congruence. Here's why congruence matters when you lead and serve other people.

1.4 Congruence Helps You Lead and Serve

We all have the same amount of time in a day. You, as a manager, need to decide:

- How much time to spend with each person you serve, your peers, and your manager.
- In what form to spend that time. For example, in a one-on-one or as part of a team.
- What to discuss with people when you do work with them.

I find the idea of congruence helpful when I think about where, when, and how I spend my time as a manager. I first read about congruence in *Software Quality Management, Vol 2: First-Order*

Measurement [WEI93]. It's a way to balance what I want (self) with the other person (other) in the context of the person and the organization.

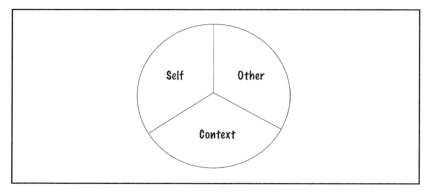

Figure 1.3: Congruence

Congruence is a way to find your balance between you and your needs, the other person and their needs, and the entire context.

If you ignore the other person, you might blame people for not working longer hours—even if they've put in a full day's or week's worth of good work. Or, you don't give them credit for the work they do.

If you ignore yourself, you might not make sure a given expert can help other people learn about their areas of expertise. You might placate or appease that person, or the people who pressure you for work by a too-early date. If you've ever seen a manager unwilling to address a team's conflict, you've probably seen placating behavior.

If you ignore the context, you might think you can use hiring shortcuts. Or, you might think that measuring time instead of outcomes is useful.

You build a culture of trust and loyalty over time, interaction by interaction. There is no shortcut to trust and loyalty.

The Buck Stops With You

Harry Truman, the 33rd U.S. President, famously had a plaque on his desk that said, "The buck stops here." It meant that the President takes responsibility for the decisions—even if he didn't implement those decisions.

The more you can take the attitude that the buck stops with you, the easier it is for people to trust you, and for you to create an environment of psychological safety. You create a support system for the people you lead and serve.

When people make mistakes, offer feedback. And, determine if you or your team needs to trap those mistakes before the mistakes occur. However, don't blame people for doing the best job they can. When you take the approach that the buck stops with you, you can create a more congruent environment.

Incongruent managers don't consider the self, the other, and the context. They don't create psychological safety. They don't generate more business value because they don't take a strategic view of the entire situation: what the business needs (the context), how they as the manager fits (the self), and the people they serve (other).

Without congruence, managers don't create a coherent and congruent work environment.

1.5 Environment Shapes Behavior

Consider Kurt Lewin's equation about a person's behavior and how the environment shapes each person's behavior and performance:

$$B = f(P, E).$$

B is a person's Behavior. That behavior is a function, f, of the Person and their Environment.

What is the environment for a person? The team, the team's culture, and the organization's culture. That environment includes:

- How the team works, in resource efficiency or flow efficiency.
- How safe the people on the team feel to discuss their concerns and challenges.
- The physical location and how the person and team use that location.
- How much trust the team members offer each other.
- How organization policies and procedures help the team perform their work.

When we look at the environment to see why a person might behave in one way or another, we can lead and serve more congruently. Especially if we want to offer change-focused feedback. We might not need the person to change—we might need to change the environment.

We create the environment—the culture—when we live our values.

1.6 Manage With Value-Based Integrity

Congruent managers live their value-based integrity:

- Honesty, which means explaining what you want and admitting when you're wrong.
- Fairness, which means balancing the needs of everyone.
- Consistency, which means we can predict that person's behaviors within some bounds.
- Truthfulness, which means helping everyone understand the true state of the situation.
- Respect others, which means creating an environment in which people can do their best work, trusting people to do a great job, and not gossiping about others.

When you serve with value-based integrity, the people you serve remember how you made them feel. When people feel good about their relationships (with their managers and colleagues), they can collaborate, act on feedback, and solve problems faster and better than you might imagine. They create their harmonic whole.

I'm not suggesting you avoid the difficult conversations—not at all. As you manage, you'll create time and space for those conversations and conduct those conversations with respect. That's part of your leadership.

To effectively lead and serve the people you manage, examine your assumptions about management.

1.7 Examine Your Management Assumptions

We all have assumptions about how to manage people. Your assumptions drive the way you think about and act as a manager—all your decisions about how you manage or serve people.

Some managers use Theory X assumptions: that people are inherently lazy and require direction. Too many organizations use Theory X in designing the organization and teams; in how they promote people; in how they assess the relative value of a person.

Some managers use Theory Y assumptions: that people want to do a great job and need an environment in which to excel with their peers. (I've paraphrased these two theories from McGregor, *The Human Side of Enterprise* [MCG06].)

In my experience, few people are either Theory X or Theory Y— they use the context of the issue to select their behaviors.

One manager, Lil, using more Theory X assumptions, said, "My people can do the work themselves but not estimate well. I do the estimation for them."

Her peer, Sue, turned and said, "The people I serve can both do the work and estimate it. I only have to explain the direction we want to go." Sue paused for a few seconds. She then continued, "I do have to check in with them a couple of times a week, but those are brief checkpoints, to make sure we still agree on the direction, the vision."

Neither manager is wrong, and neither is right. Lil was new to the organization, serving several teams of people who haven't estimated anything on their own for years. They were afraid of estimating "wrong," so they padded their estimates. Note that fear played a huge role in their behaviors.

Sue, on the other hand, had spent the previous three years reinforcing everyone's interdependence as teams, and the fact that when teams worked together, everyone won. The people were not afraid of the work or the estimates. They were more concerned about staying focused on the right direction, which is why Sue checked in with them regularly.

Both managers assessed the context before deciding how to lead and serve the people.

Your management assumptions will shape the culture you create.

1.8 Managers Create and Refine the Culture

When managers lead and serve others, they create or refine the culture and the environment, the system of work. Culture bounds your organization's system of work—the environment.

Edgar Schein in *Organizational Culture and Leadership* [SCH10] says that our artifacts, values, and assumptions define our culture. When I consider a culture, I can boil it down to these three ideas:

- How do we treat each other?
- What can we discuss?
- What do we reward?

When I use that lens to think about culture, I can see a given organization's culture more clearly. That's why every organization's culture is different.

Managers reinforce the culture when they offer reinforcing feedback for the "best" behaviors and offer change-focused feedback for the "worst." You may have seen this Gruenert and Whitaker quote:

> The Culture of any organization is shaped by the worst behavior the leader is willing to tolerate." —Steve Gruenert and Todd Whitaker, *School Culture Rewired*, ch. 3 (2015)

Cultures are not wrong or bad. The culture will determine how well—or not well—the organization works.

Every action you take—or don't—adds to the culture. Other people see how you treat people; what and how you discuss; and what you publicly recognize and reward. Even if you think you're not intentionally creating the culture, you are.

The less you think about culture, the more likely you are to create a culture you don't want.

A big part of any culture is how safe people feel to do the work. Aside from psychological safety, people feel safe when you, as a manager, serve with value-based integrity.

Managers can lead and serve others when they see the system of work—the people, the products and services, and how those people work together.

1.9 Consider These Principles to Lead and Serve Others

When managers lead and serve others, they adapt the principles in these ways:

1. Clarify the team's purpose so the team can know and focus on the highest value work. As a manager, you provide value by creating an environment that makes it possible for people to do their best work.
2. Build empathy with the people who do the work. When you acknowledge people's contributions outside the team, they realize why the work was important.

3. Build a safe environment. Your job might be to protect the team from organizational mayhem.

4. Seek outcomes and optimize for the overarching goal. Successful knowledge work arises from a harmonic whole—flow efficiency.

5. Encourage experiments and learning. The more people learn together, the better they can make their environment. They can improve a little every day.

6. Catch people succeeding. When people hear what they've done well, they are more likely to consider what else they might improve.

7. Exercise your value-based integrity as a model for the people you lead and serve.

You'll notice I didn't include transparency or communication in these principles. That's because if you use all these principles, you will communicate more effectively. You will be as transparent as you can be with the people you serve.

You create an environment where people can do their best work.

Given these principles, consider how you build your leadership excellence.

1.10 Lead and Serve with Excellence

Management excellence combines these principles with the idea of a harmonic whole. I've succeeded when I ask myself these questions:

- How can I feel safe and help others feel safe as they do the work? Safety encourages open conversation.
- How can I extend trust so people feel as if they can deliver to the best of their abilities?
- How can I build collaboration into the culture?

If I explain the outcomes I want and then ask myself these questions, I tend to exhibit more management excellence.

I'm not asking you to change your beliefs. Your beliefs arise from the results of your actions and interactions with others. Change your behaviors as an experiment. Then, you can decide if you want to change your beliefs and then, the culture.

You don't need to be perfect. If you can explain when you experiment, people will build empathy, trust, and respect with you.

Become a modern manager and build ease in how you lead and serve, especially to create that harmonic whole, where the team succeeds.

Let's start.

CHAPTER 2

How Many People Can You Serve as a Manager?

Many executives think it's easy for first-level managers to manage more than nine people.

In my first management role, I "managed" one person. That person didn't need much management. He taught me how to manage capable people like him. He saved me from making too many mistakes. That experience was terrific practice for me.

Later in my management career, I managed a "team" of 15 testers. They were not a team. They were a group because they worked independently from each other on different projects. We were a team only for learning about testing.

I didn't think of my role as allocating people to projects, because most people remained on long-standing product teams. I managed the project portfolio for the test group, so I could match-make testers to products.

What else did I do as a manager?

- Conducted one-on-ones with each person, some weekly, some biweekly. But I had a private conversation with each person at least every two weeks. I discussed career development with each person at every one-on-one.
- Conducted a weekly learning meeting where everyone in the test group would learn something. This was a community of practice meeting. Sometimes it was about professional practices. Sometimes it was about tools. Sometimes it was about project management techniques. The group decided what they wanted

to learn. I greased the skids and facilitated their learning. People took turns presenting something. Yes, I did too. Sometimes, we invited other people across the company to present. We had a long list of things to learn.

- I made sure everyone knew what everyone else was doing. But not with a serial status meeting. I took people's email status to me, collated it, and emailed it to everyone. If anyone was interested, they could read it. If not, they could trash it. The idea was that since they were all working on different projects, they might discover insights someone else might want to know. I knew I was no longer technical enough to solve their problems for them. I could facilitate their problem solving, if necessary. I provided information they might not have. They could follow up.
- I made sure that the right people were invited to the right meetings. This was more difficult than it sounds. I did not want to go to all the meetings. But I was invited. I had to get uninvited, make sure the right testers were invited, get off the email list, and make sure the testers were on the list.
- I generated job analyses for all the open positions, phone screened candidates, and arranged the interviewing.

I'm sure there was more, but that's what I remember now.

I recently met a smart CTO of a company with about 100 engineers. He said he wanted a flat organization. That makes sense to me. Then he said, "Every engineering manager should be able to manage about 15-20 engineers and the projects that they work on, too."

Oh, boy. You will notice that I was not managing projects in my list above. I had full days with just my management responsibilities. Even with that, I worked after dinner. I conducted phone screens and wrote reports. I worked after dinner because I had no time during the day.

Could I have done any useful project management? No. Could I have managed any more people? No. Certainly not up to 20 people. Why? Because I needed time to meet with everyone, some people each week.

Why could I manage 15 people? Because, by this time, I was an experienced manager. I already had management practice. First with one person. Then with three or four. Then seven, eight.

When I served nine people, I realized I had to move to biweekly one-on-ones for some people. I asked the people who were more senior if they minded. No, it was okay. But if all nine people were more junior and needed coaching? It would have been a disaster. (At the time, I didn't know about mobbing and how fast a team learns when they work together.) By the time I served 15 people, I had some idea of what to do so I could serve them all.

No one can manage an "infinite" number of people and do a great job.

It's the same principle as code or projects.

If you don't care how good the code is, you can write as much code as you want. If you don't care how good your project management is, you can manage as many projects as you want. If you don't care how good your management is, you can "manage" as many people as you want.

Everyone has their own point where they no longer can be effective as a manager. For me, that number was 15 already fairly capable people. Maybe you can manage more people than I did, especially if the managers serve autonomous teams. When teams understand how to manage themselves, the manager doesn't need to do much for a given team.

And, if the teams you serve are not autonomous? You have too much work.

The problem with too much work is this: you can't think faster or harder. Each of us has some limit to how well we can think. If we don't learn how to work differently, we can't "scale" what we do.

The more the teams manage themselves, the less management the teams need. That's why I recommend you Encourage Flow Efficiency on page 2. The teams might need your help to remove impediments.

Great managers offer feedback and coaching. They might offer meta-feedback and meta-coaching if a person wants to discuss how they develop their interpersonal skills. Once the teams know how to offer feedback and coaching to each other, managers can focus up, at the level of the team, not for each person.

Great managers create a culture of learning. That means they create and offer a learning environment for the people, a place for people to learn. I expected the people in my group to spend the rest of their time learning on their own and being responsible.

And, great managers build a trusting relationship with each person. That's the point of the one-on-one.

Because we were hiring, and because I had responsibilities across the organization, we were *all* busy. If I hadn't made time for our one-on-ones, I could have gone for weeks, not seeing people. That would have been Wrong.

How much do the people on the team need *you* as their manager? Can they manage their interpersonal relationships? What about their decisions? How many decisions can they make without you?

Back in Book 1, I suggested you, as a manager, learn to delegate. The more the team or group can manage their interpersonal relationships, the more satisfied the people will be. The more people know what to expect of you, the more they can build their relationships with each other.

Management is not about micromanagement. It's about creating an environment in which everyone can do their best work. If you are too busy to do that, are you really managing?

2.1 Myth: You Can Manage Any Number of People as a Manager

"Cindy, I need to add three more people to your team." Patrick, the CTO, leaned in the doorway. He turned, about to walk away.

"Wait a sec. We need to discuss this. You don't get to drop that bombshell and leave. Why do you want me to hire more people?" Cindy looked concerned.

"No, I don't want you to hire anyone," Patrick said. "I'm moving them over from Tranh's team. He's not coaching them well. You coach your team well. He's not. I want you to manage them."

"If you give me three more people, I won't be able to coach them properly. I won't have time," Cindy replied. "You don't want me to make team leads, which I don't understand. I'll have twelve people, which is too many. No. I don't want them. Give them to someone else or let me manage my team the way I want."

Patrick walked in and sat down. 'What do you mean, 'manage the way you want'? I don't interfere with you."

Cindy snorted. "Sure, you do. You have all kinds of rules. I can't have team leads. I must have a minimum of three people to manage. I must write code, no matter how many people I manage or what else I'm doing for you."

Patrick said, "Well, that's how I managed."

"You didn't use an agile approach. In fact, you were the Big Boss of the Code," Cindy said. "You're working off old data. None of your rules make sense in an agile organization. None of this helps me manage the project portfolio or provide coaching or career development or the kind of feedback that makes sense. Your rules don't help me help the product owners or the program managers. They don't help me work on the architectural decisions for where the product is going—even though I only facilitate those decisions."

Patrick frowned.

"I only have one-on-ones biweekly with my team," Cindy said. "I don't have time for more than that. And I don't have time for any more management work. You don't have time to meet with me. You keep canceling our one-on-ones. When you're free, I'm not."

Patrick said, "I'm pretty busy."

"So am I!" Cindy said. "And my 'team' isn't just one team. It's two cross-functional teams. I work with the testers as well as the developers. I don't know how to coach the BAs that well, so I don't. So, no—no, thank you," Cindy concluded. "I am up to my eyeballs. I can't manage more people without relaxing some of your rules. I don't want to manage any more people. Give them to someone else."

2.2 What Do First-Line Managers Do?

I wish there was a consensus on what first-line managers do. There isn't even a consensus on the title for these folks. Some first-line managers are managers. Some are called leads. Some managers code or test if they are functional managers for development or test teams, even in an agile environment.

For some teams, their manager is the way they learn "how to do things here." They have not learned that team approaches to the work, such as pairing or a buddy system or swarming or mob programming is just as effective, if not more, than manager-led coaching. Why? Because that's how their manager learned. And their manager, the current director or senior manager, got that promotion because he or she was the most valuable technical person.

Avoid filling a first-line manager's day so the manager can learn how to lead and serve well. When the first-line manager has sufficient slack in his or her day, the manager can take time to build those necessary relationships with the people. These relationships are a great way to know if people are satisfied at work.

And, if a first-line manager is busy doing the work, how can the manager learn to delegate work and responsibility to someone else?

2.3 How Managers Serve Others

Here's a possible list of the ways managers can serve the people they lead:

- Creating space for one-on-ones at least once every other week. See Gather Data With One-on-Ones on page 30.
- Discuss the person's career progression.
- Offer reinforcing feedback.
- Offer feedback and coaching, or meta-feedback and meta-coaching.

- Ask about the kind of training people want and facilitate that training.
- Create and support Communities of Practice.

Managers serve their teams—and across the organization—by creating an environment where people can collaborate and learn with others. That learning will require experiments.

Start with the ideas in Consider These Principles for Leading and Serving Others on page 15. Decide how you can use those principles in your environment.

2.4 What's a Reasonable Number of People to Manage?

As always, with a juicy question like that, the answer is, "It depends." It depends on how seasoned the manager is, the kind of process the team uses, and how much or little the team manages itself.

If the first-line manager is learning how to be a manager, the manager needs to practice with fewer people. Why? The manager needs to learn how to avoid interfering in the work. That's difficult enough with three or four people. It's close to impossible if a new manager has more people because the temptation to insert yourself into all decisions is impossible to resist.

My experience is that we have challenges when teams reach multiples of three. If you're a new manager and you practice, you can learn to manage a team of three people pretty quickly. You might even be able to learn to serve up to six people pretty fast.

But, something happens once you need to serve more than nine people.

When you try to serve nine people, you might not have enough time for one-on-ones. If the "team" is matrixed onto several projects, you attempt to serve people who work in different environments.

You don't serve one team. You're seeing the system and trying to manage the impediments for several teams.

What if you have 18-21 people on a team? Sorry, that's not a team with one goal and interdependent work. It's several teams. Even if they're all on one program or product, they are not all on one feature set. As soon as they work on multiple feature sets, they have different goals.

And, yes, you can serve those roughly 20 people, assuming they manage themselves most of the time. By that, I mean they:

- Know how and do offer each other feedback and coaching on a regular basis.
- Know how to create team consensus around various decisions. They understand how to progress as a team.
- Know how to trust each other to deliver the work.

Each of these knowledge areas means that people have learned or can learn. When should you consciously create learning opportunities?

2.5 **Create Learning Opportunities**

I meet too many people who are bored in their jobs. The people early in their career say, "I'm ready for more responsibility. I want more challenges. But there's nowhere to go. My manager won't let me learn. My manager keeps me under his thumb."

Too many people later in the careers say, "The Manager already architected or implemented a proof of concept. I don't have to think. All I do is code/test/whatever to their spec."

That's no way to work.

When I ask managers why they do this, the managers tell me, "I must maintain my technical skills."

You, as a manager, can maintain a level of technical skills that does not require you to be in the code or the tests or the UI, or whatever your area of expertise is. I recommend the team or workgroup learn together, whenever possible. I'll talk more about this in Book 3.

People deserve a chance to grow and learn. One of your jobs as a manager is to facilitate their learning. The first action you might consider is removing your expertise from their work.

2.6 Remove Yourself as the Expert

Many first-line managers see themselves as the expert, as the sole source of knowledge for their group. You may have started as the expert. However, as soon as you become a manager, start moving out of that expert's seat. You can't be the expert for the team. And, if you Encourage Flow Efficiency on page 2, you'll resist the temptation to create experts. (See Do Experts Help Finish the Work? on page 135 for more on this topic.)

Spread the expertise love. Ask people to work together. This is easy on an agile team, where people are likely to pair, swarm, or mob on features. If you don't have an agile team, ask who is interested in acquiring new knowledge.

Remember, unless you have a toxic environment, people want to learn new skills. If no one wants to learn what you know, that is information for you. Maybe your expertise is outdated, or the workplace is hostile, or people are already looking for other jobs. Use your one-on-ones to determine what's going on.

2.7 Build Trusting Relationships With Your Team

Your management position, first-line or not, is about building trusting relationships. The more people you manage, the more time you need to spend building relationships based on trust. What other deliverables does your organization request of you?

Every manager balances the leading and serving of each various team member with the other work. For example, if you're supposed to deliver customer presentations every day, when do you have time for one-on-ones?

I see too many first-line managers who are supposed to serve more than 10 people, and contribute technically, and participate in product decisions. When you're stretched, how can you serve the people you lead?

While this affects first-line managers more than it affects more senior managers, it's a management problem. It requires problem solving and leadership. And that problem-solving is what management is for, right?

2.8 **Focus on Serving, Not Controlling**

Too often, I see senior managers who want to maintain a flat organization because they don't want too many "direct reports." That's reasonable. It's not wise to ask people to manage more people than they can.

If you desire a flat organization, make sure you help everyone develop trusting relationships with each other. You create a culture in which people can learn. These ideas work well when you Encourage Flow Efficiency on page 2. Resource efficiency is incongruent with a flat organization—resource efficiency doesn't fit the context of a flat organization. Resource efficiency requires more people who direct the work of other people.

Flow efficiency is congruent with a flat organization and managers who serve the people they lead. Flow efficiency helps teams become autonomous and self-managing.

If you're a senior manager, make sure you aren't asking another manager to control other people's actions. That's Theory X management. Worse, you won't get the outcomes you want.

2.9 **Options to Lead and Serve**

Consider these options to lead and serve the people in your team or group:

- Make sure you conduct one-on-ones with people often enough to learn what they want to do.
- Assuming you have that kind of work available for people, identify what the person needs to learn.
- With the person, create an action plan that helps the person succeed in that role.
- Encourage the team to work together, as much as possible. That will help you avoid being the expert. And, the team will learn how to learn together.

CHAPTER 3

How Often Do You Meet Privately With People?

Everyone deserves a private time and place to speak with their manager. They need this time to be regular and frequent—at least once every two weeks.

As a manager, you need one-on-ones to build and reinforce a trusting relationship. You use the one-on-one to reinforce what people are doing well. You offer time for practice and discussion for how the other person might offer feedback or coaching to his or her peers. You might offer feedback and coaching to the person directly, depending on the context.

And, when you have a freewheeling discussion, you help people see what's important to you and to the organization. People will see how they can add value. They will make better decisions as they proceed.

Just as important, you can learn what's going on in the organization. The one-on-one offers a variety of ways to see and hear through other people.

Back when I was a manager, I asked for rumors in both team meetings and in the one-on-ones. I wanted to use other people to help me manage my blind spots. I found that question useful to inject a little humor at times and to tell me what was going on.

Everyone deserves sacrosanct one-on-one time.

3.1 Myth: I Don't Need One-on-Ones

I was working with a client on the organization's project portfolio, the order of which projects they were going to do when, and which projects they were not going to staff for now. Stan, the engineering director, was convinced he knew exactly who was working on what. I was equally convinced he did not.

I had inside information—some of the developers told me they were working on skunkworks projects, projects that people had started out of their initiative to see if they had any value.

"I know what the people in my group are doing, Johanna. Each and every one of them."

"But you have twenty-five people in your group, Stan," I protested.

"And I walk around and see what every single person is doing. I read their check-ins, too. I know what they are doing."

Even if you read all the check-ins—and that's a form of micromanagement—you don't know if people are happy or sad, satisfied, or ready to walk out the door. Or, if they're coaching others. Or if they want to learn something specific. Or, worse, if you have a systemic problem that will cause all of them to quit in the next three months.

You have no data about the people. One-on-ones help you gather data of all kinds.

3.2 Gather Data With One-on-Ones

One-on-ones help you gather a variety of information. Some of that information is about the person—what's working for them and what's not. What they want out of their career and what they don't. When they need feedback or coaching, even if that doesn't come from you.

One-on-ones are a great time to offer reinforcing feedback, where you catch people doing something great. They can build on their strengths.

Regular one-on-ones help you see how much each person trusts the rest of the team. And, if the person still engages with the purpose of the organization. As you build trust with the person, you'll learn about their ability to do great work and the impediments you need to remove.

One-on-ones aren't for status reports, especially if you're trying to use agile approaches in your organization. They aren't just for knowing about all the projects.

One-on-ones allow you to fine-tune the organization. You can see small problems before they get big. You can see interpersonal problems before they create a storm. You can offer a safe place to practice a person's feedback to another (meta feedback) or coaching to another (meta coaching).

If you are a manager and you aren't using one-on-ones, you are not using the most important management tool you have.

3.3 Model Behavior and Feedback in One-on-Ones

I do like to know what people are thinking. And, I never recommend any manager read check-in comments for code or tests as a way to know what people complete. I also don't recommend reading any of the tickets in whatever tool people might use.

But if you ask a developer if she has any great ideas for the next release of a new product or the next release of that product people hadn't considered, you invite the developer to think strategically. You can substitute tester, business analyst, writer, or anyone else in that sentence.

One of the most valuable conversations I had as a manager was back when I was managing a test group. During a one-on-one, Drew, one of the junior testers said, "JR, we are doing this all wrong."

Disconcerted, I asked, "How so?"

Drew said, "We are looking at this product in the wrong way. Here, let me show you another way to slice and dice this." He drew pictures on my whiteboard of the way we were testing and then drew more pictures. He was right. We were testing in a way that didn't expose enough risks.

"Wow, I'm really glad you told me now. But why did you wait until our one-on-one? I wish you'd said something when we kicked off the testing last week."

"Well, Steve is the senior tester on the project, right?" Drew asked. I nodded.

He continued. "I wasn't sure how he would take it. I'm pretty junior compared to him. I didn't want him to take it the wrong way. I wanted to run it by you. And, this way, I get to check it with you first."

I received excellent feedback in that conversation:

- I was not eliciting enough options from everyone on the team.
- I was not creating an environment where everyone could offer each other feedback.

I was able to model the behavior where Drew coached me.

Later, Drew asked me how to offer feedback to other people on the team. Because we had already built trust, he could practice his words with me.

It doesn't matter if you serve more traditional or agile teams. In general, people are aware of the implied hierarchy. These people might need assurance that their ideas are sound. That's why having a one-on-one with a senior person helps. They need the reassurance and the self-esteem that arises from the feedback they receive from bouncing their ideas off someone else.

3.4 Privacy for Private Problems

You also need one-on-ones to manage private issues. The people in your organizations have families and private lives. They have spouses or significant others, children, parents, homes, pets, and other responsibilities outside of work. Sometimes they need time to manage their lives outside of work. I've learned of wonderful and tragic events in one-on-ones.

One woman told me she had an upset stomach for months. She'd gone to specialist after specialist over a period of a couple of months.

In our regular one-on-one, she told me she was taking the entire Friday off for a battery of tests to see what was wrong. She just couldn't take it anymore and needed to get to the bottom of the problem. I wished her well and told her the company and I were behind her.

She left me a voicemail on Friday night telling me she was six and a half months pregnant. Her husband left me a voicemail on Sunday night telling me she had delivered a daughter and that both the mom and daughter were fine. He sounded shell-shocked.

We all celebrated their good news.

In another one-on-one, a developer told me he was taking off Tuesday and Thursday afternoons indefinitely.

I said, "I can clear your Tuesday and Thursday afternoons for a couple of weeks. But sooner or later the team is going to wonder. I'm going to have to tell somebody something, so, I'd rather you tell me now and we can figure out what to say. Can you explain why?"

"No," he said, as he started to cry.

I pushed my tissues across the desk. "What are these for?" he asked.

"You're crying," I explained.

"I am? No way." He protested.

"Yes, you are. You might want to use a tissue. If you don't want to tell me more, that's OK. But I think there's something serious going on in your life, and you might need more help than a box of tissues."

He took a tissue and blew his nose.

I continued. "We have an Employee Assistance Program that might help, even if you don't want my help. I'll leave for a few minutes if you like. You can compose yourself, and when I return, we can talk about it, or maybe you can go to HR, or you can go back to work."

I left for a few minutes and got us both water. When I returned, he had stopped crying and was ready to talk.

He explained his wife had just been diagnosed with breast cancer. She was going for chemo on Tuesday and Thursday afternoons for six weeks and then they were going to see how the cancer was doing.

"I can work with this," I said. "We don't have to touch your vacation or anything. We can make sure you are on full salary. I can make this work."

"You can?" He sounded incredulous.

"Sure, this kind of situation is why they pay me the Big Bucks."

He grinned. "You already told me I make more than you do."

I smiled. "Yup, and you're worth it. Now, let me address this with HR and when you're ready, let's discuss this with the team."

He took a big breath in and released it slowly. "Okay. I'm ready now."

Without one-on-ones, I would not have learned of these challenges. I couldn't have helped. I wouldn't have had enough information to create a resilient and adaptable organization.

In my experience, many people don't publicize the Big Bad Things in their lives in public. Too often, they suffer in silence. (Some people do publicize those problems, and sometimes, their teams support them.) The developer who supported his wife through her cancer treatments could have asked his team for support and they would have supported him. He didn't feel comfortable asking for that support.

People might have Big Wonderful Things, too, such as taking time off for a teen's prom or finalizing an adoption, or any of the wonderful events we have.

If the team isn't yet psychologically safe with each other, or if they don't yet have enough trust, you serve the team by working through the issues privately with the person with the Big Thing.

That's why everyone needs regular private time with a responsible manager.

3.5 One-on-Ones Allow the Manager to Serve

Managers serve the people in their teams. That service might take the form of coaching or explaining the purpose or the strategy. That service might mean you, as a manager, have access to information, or who to approach to accomplish something.

While I assisted the gentleman supporting his wife to organize his workdays and time, I didn't do it from a parental stance. I worked as a peer. I happened to have access to information he didn't. I knew what we, as a company, were willing to do in these kinds of situations.

The manager represents the organization to the employee. This is not a parent-child relationship; this is a peer-to-peer relationship.

I have learned from "my" employees. I put quotes around the word "my" because they aren't *mine*. They are employees of the organization. They are human beings who do not belong to me but do affiliate with me. My status in the organization doesn't depend on how many people I "have."

If your status does depend on the people you "have," consider how you can help your team or teams succeed at generating valuable outcomes for your organization. You might find that your ability to create a successful environment matters more than the people you "have."

One thing matters to me: that all the people I serve are able to perform to their maximum capability. If I can enhance their capability, if I can leverage their work, then I have performed my job as a manager. That says to me I need to serve my staff.

"My" people are the people I support and serve.

3.6 Build the Relationship with One-on-Ones

I don't see how you can serve people without getting to know them. I'm not suggesting you insinuate your way into their families or other relationships. But, what do people enjoy doing at work? What do they think their strengths are? What do they want to learn? What kinds of things stop them from finishing work that matters? Do they feel underutilized or undervalued?

Those are the kinds of questions managers can ask to serve people.

While you might learn more about people's families over time, I recommend getting to know the person at *work*.

A bad relationship—or no relationship—with a manager may well push people away from the organization.

When you have one-on-ones with the people you serve, you can build trusting relationships with them. Back in Book 1, I suggested each manager conduct a 20-30 minute one-on-one every week or two.

You can serve people by helping them—if they want your help—with career development, coaching, and mentoring. You can offer feedback if you catch people doing something great or if you notice them doing something not so great. And, because you know what people are working on, you can manage the project portfolio and know when it's time to hire people.

One-on-ones becomes another way to gather data.

3.7 Structure Your One-on-Ones

When I conduct one-on-ones, I prepare in two ways: with a way to take notes and with a structure.

I either have a physical notebook per person or a file folder for each person. I happen to prefer a file folder because I can more easily lock the folders in one drawer. I don't have to fumble, looking for the right notebook.

I don't recommend taking notes on an electronic device. First, I don't want to create a barrier between us. Second, I worry about other people changing permissions on my private files. I know I can lock the paper away and know the paper is private.

These are my preferences for note-taking. You'll decide what works for you, not just for notes, but for the structure.

I structure one-on-ones in one of several ways. This first outline is a general-purpose structure:

1. Greeting.
2. Review any ongoing action items (your action items).
3. Ask for obstacles/challenges/impediments.
4. Any help/feedback/coaching they want.
5. Career development placeholder. (You might not discuss their career every week. This is in the outline so you don't forget.)

6. Ask if they have anything they want to discuss.

7. Review any new action items (yours and theirs).

If you're not using an agile approach, you might need to ask about their status for their work.

As you each become more comfortable with each other, consider evolving your one-on-one structure to more of a pull system for you, as a manager:

1. *From* a Greeting *to* a Check-in. (A check-in is one word or a phrase that explains your mental state.)

2. *From* Your Agenda *to* the Other Person's Agenda. As part of the agenda, consider:

   • Obstacles

   • Help/feedback/coaching

   • Career development

   • Action item review

You might even like the "minimal" one-on-one a client shared with me:

• Check-in

• Do you need anything? (Not just from you, anything at all.)

• Is anything getting in your way?

• What can I, as your manager, do to help?

Several of my clients who practiced pull one-on-ones for a while now ask the person to take the responsibility to create the agenda. Then, as a manager, you ask this one question: "What's on your agenda?"

If the person asks you a question you don't know the answer to, do say, "I don't know," and add that to your personal kanban board. (See Book 1 for a discussion of when *you* need help.)

The longer you practice one-on-ones, the more comfortable you will be deciding which structure makes sense for you—and the person you serve.

If you haven't experienced one-on-ones, consider reading *Behind Closed Doors: Secrets of Great Management* [BCD05] to see one-on-ones in action.

3.8 Decide When to Conduct One-on-Ones

I'm convinced that all managers have too many meetings. I hope you don't. However, the more meetings you have, the more trouble you'll have making time to conduct regular one-on-ones. You'll need to balance the time you need to think, the other meetings you have, and the thinking time the people you serve need.

You might not have considered these three pieces of scheduling your one-on-ones until now. Paul Graham articulated this in his discussion about the cost of meetings to programmers. See Maker's Schedule, Manager's Schedule.[1]

You might have time early in the day. And, if the people you serve also have time then, that might be a good time to meet.

However, let's imagine this scenario. You have Tuesday mornings available. The team doesn't start working together until 10 A.M.

You conduct three one-on-ones, starting at 8:30 A.M. If you continue the one-on-ones—even though you have the time, you destroy the team's flow efficiency starting at 10 A.M.

What if you have no other time during the week for the one-on-ones? Reduce your other meetings.

The more management responsibilities I had, the fewer technical meetings I participated in. I used the advice in Remove Yourself as the Expert on page 27. I often discovered I was no longer the right person for several meetings. That realization opened my schedule to other options.

What if you manage managers? Do the ideas in Graham's essay about the cost of a meeting still apply? Yes and no.

When managers multitask by design, they have more meetings. Those meetings interfere with the managers' time to think. When I

---

[1] http://www.paulgraham.com/makersschedule.html

served managers, I wanted them to think, not just react. I Encourage Flow Efficiency on page 2 for the managers, too. I'll discuss this more in Book 3.

Ask people what works for them to find 20-30 minutes once a week with you. How can you find a good time to meet with people, so you build that relationship and so neither of you feels interrupted?

3.9 What If You Don't Have Time for One-on-Ones?

Some managers think they don't have time for one-on-ones. They miss out on the single most valuable management tool if they stop having one-on-ones.

If you're too busy doing technical work, please read Book 1. Make sure you fulfill your management responsibilities first before you fulfill any technical responsibilities. Why? Because managers leverage everyone else's work.

Prioritize your one-on-ones to be the *most* important work you do all week. Your one-on-ones will enable you to create relationships with people you need to trust, recognize organizational impediments, and observe early warning signs and signals for future problems.

3.10 Options to Organize Your One-on-Ones

Consider these options for your one-on-ones:

1. Find time to meet with each person at least biweekly, if not weekly. Beware of cutting into people's thinking time. Ask people *when* you can meet with them—and make it a time you both want.

2. Review Structure Your One-on-Ones on page 36 to see how you would like to structure your one-on-ones to start and then evolve.

3. You might receive feedback and coaching in your one-on-ones, as I did above. If so, know that you are already building an environment of trust.

CHAPTER 4

Do I Really Need to Tell Someone How They're Doing?

A couple of years into my career, my manager gave me great feedback. At my annual review—three months late—he told me I got projects almost all the way done. I got them to 96%, 97%, maybe even 99%. I didn't quite finish them.

I was disappointed but happy to know I could work on something specific. I asked him, "Oh, the project I finished last month?"

"No," he said. "All the projects since you've been here."

"All eight projects?" I asked. "All of them?"

"Afraid so," he said.

"Why did you wait so long to tell me? I could have improved. How was I supposed to know?" I asked. I was quite frustrated.

Both my manager and I learned something that day.

People can't just "know" how they're doing. You need to tell them. Clearly, respectfully, as a peer. But they do need to know.

When people receive feedback, they understand their performance.

4.1 Myth: People Should Just Know How They're Doing

Margaret, a manager, was concerned about one of her employees, Chad. She met with her manager, Peter, to discuss the problem.

"Chad just isn't cutting it," Margaret said. "He's not finishing anything on time, and what he does finish is full of defects. His attitude is so bad that no one wants to work with him. I guess I'll have to let him go."

"I hate to see you do that. He's been productive up until the last couple of months," Peter said. "Have you told Chad about these problems?"

"Well, I told him I was disappointed with his work."

"But have you given him specific feedback?"

"Telling him I'm disappointed isn't specific?" Margaret asked, frowning.

Peter paused for a moment and replied, "Saying you're disappointed is not useful feedback. If I told you I was disappointed in your management of Chad, you wouldn't know what I was disappointed about. I'd create a parent-child dynamic, instead of a collegial relationship between adults at work. I'd reduce your trust in me because I'd be treating you more like a child than an adult. That dynamic would persist even after I give you specific examples."

Margaret cocked her head. "Oh?"

Peter nodded. "You'll need to give Chad specific and recent examples of the work or behavior you want to change," he said. "Are you going to tell him what to do, or are you willing to solve the problems jointly?"

"We'll work out the answers together," replied Margaret.

"Your big challenge is to construct the feedback so that Chad can hear it. Feel free to ask me for help," said Peter.

Margaret had three issues to discuss with Chad: late deliverables, defects in his deliverables, and his attitude. She had specific instances of Chad's late deliverables and his defects, but she needed to identify the specific behaviors he had exhibited that led her to conclude that he had a bad attitude.

Margaret constructed the feedback message by first creating an opening to talk. Next, she would describe the behavior or results she had seen, stating the impact in ways that affected her personally. Finally, she would make a request for change.

Margaret prepared talking points. By writing a script, she wouldn't be flustered when it was time to talk to Chad. She wouldn't actually use the script when speaking with him. She was sure the meeting would differ from the script, but the script would help her to identify the issues she wanted to address and ways to phrase the feedback.

Since Margaret hadn't been giving Chad feedback regularly, she needed to be careful about creating an opening. When she was ready to talk to Chad, she stopped by his office and said, "Chad, I'd like to have a conversation about how we work together. I haven't discussed feedback with you very well. I owe you more feedback. And, I bet you have feedback for me, too. If you have time now, I'm happy to chat immediately. But if you're in the middle of something, Wednesday at 1:30 works just as well."

Chad replied, "Sure, now is great. Let me grab my notebook. Your office?"

She nodded and they walked to her office together.

He sat, put down his notebook, and said, "I know you have feedback to give me, but there's something I need to let you know first. I've been really unhappy in the last couple of months. I really dislike this work. When can I finish this and move to that other project?"

Margaret was surprised. She then realized what had happened. Because Chad disliked the work, he was dragging his feet and not performing up to his usual standards.

She adjusted her original script and focused on the problem at hand.

"I'm really glad you told me this," she said. "I wasn't aware of your dissatisfaction, but I have noticed that your work hasn't been up to its usual standards—your last three deliverables were late, and the testers found more than twenty defects in your code over the past couple of weeks. When your work is late and has more defects—and I don't know about it in advance—I can't plan the project work very well. Were you aware of these problems?"

"Yeah, I'm having trouble staying focused," Chad said. "I really hate this work."

"Why didn't you tell me?"

"You're always so busy, and you kept canceling our one-on-ones, so I thought you didn't want to talk to me."

"Oh," Margaret said. "Thank you for telling me. I didn't realize you'd take that message away from my canceling our one-on-ones. I've been plowed under the last couple of months. But let's get back to you. I still need you to finish this project work for the next month. Can you?"

"As long as we timebox it, I can stay more focused and finish it. I was thinking I'd ask Jonathan and Kim for help with review. If I know someone's going to read my code, I tend to do a better job," Chad said. "But when can I move to the other project? It's just what I like to do."

"I can't move you until this work is complete. I need you to do the best job you can on your current project and stay focused. But maybe I can help by meeting with you more regularly. Do you want to meet more often than once a week?"

"How about if we meet twice next week? You can keep me on the straight and narrow while I muddle through this piece. Then we can move back to once a week."

Margaret smiled and felt her shoulders relax. "Great, you've got a deal," she said. "Now, let's talk about another problem. In meetings, I've seen you fight with people about things I didn't think you even cared about. I was quite surprised you called Brian brain-dead. We don't call people names here. What's up with that?"

"I think Brian's design is brain-dead," Chad said. "What else am I supposed to say?"

"You can disagree with a design choice anytime," Margaret said. "We want to be able to discuss how to make the product better. However, you called Brian a name and shamed him in front of the entire team. When you do that, people stop trusting you. No more name-calling. I don't like calling a design brain-dead, either. What's wrong with saying, 'I'm worried about these aspects of the design?'"

Chad shrugged. "Nothing, I guess." He paused. "Well, I think it would be better than just telling him I don't like it."

"We disagree with all kinds of things at work all the time," Margaret said. "We need to discuss how to make the work stronger. But, disagreeing isn't the same as name-calling." She paused. "I'm sorry we haven't met regularly. But, we have a culture of treating each other with respect here. When you call people names, you're not treating them with respect. Do you know what to do instead?"

Chad said, "Well, I guess I could say, 'I don't like that design.' Would that work?"

"Maybe," Margaret said. "How about if you acknowledge what you do like about the design and then explain your concerns? And, if you do have ideas, you could add them. After you acknowledge and explain first."

Chad said, "How would that work?"

"You could say, 'I see where you're going with this design. I'm concerned that this design will make a lot of work for all of us,' and then explain why. When you explain the design or code problems, people will listen. They won't listen if you call anyone names."

"That's a good tip," Chad said. "I'll try it next time. I wish more designers thought like programmers."

"They can when we all work together," Margaret said. "In our next one-on-one, let's practice. If you want, we can try role-playing or find some resources together."

"Yes, that would help me," Chad said. "Thanks."

Chad and Margaret met regularly for the next few weeks. In the end, Chad returned to being the dependable developer Margaret had once known. He mended his relationships with the other team members and strengthened his working relationship with Margaret.

Margaret, in turn, gained insight into the kind of work Chad would enjoy and do well. Feedback, not firing, was the answer.

4.2 Manage Your Feedback Words

There are two types of feedback: reinforcing feedback and change-focused feedback. Reinforcing feedback is not a compliment. Change-focused feedback is not criticism.

They are:

Information, delivered in the present about the recent past, with the hope of influencing the future. —Definition of feedback from What Did You Say? The Art of Giving and Receiving Feedback [SSW97].

We evaluate when we use the words "compliment" or "criticize." The most useful feedback does not evaluate. It offers information. We use reinforcing feedback when we want the person to repeat either this action or a similar action.

We use change-focused feedback when that behavior wasn't what we wanted for some reason.

It's all feedback at work. We don't lead or serve "subordinates" or children. We lead and serve adults. Let's treat them like adults.

You might also use appreciations, a form of a personalized thank you. An appreciation takes this form:

I appreciate you, the-persons-name, for the-thing-you-did-or-didn't-do. It affected me in this way.

Appreciations are a special form of reinforcing feedback. While I was out sick, one of the people I served made several serious decisions. I had delegated the decisions to her, and she extended her responsibility in ways neither of us expected.

She was a little nervous when I returned. What would I think?

I was thrilled. I said something like this, "I appreciate you, Jen, for making that decision in such a timely manner. You saved us as a department from having difficult conversations with a Very Important Customer. You saved me a ton of time. I appreciate your transparency and willingness to make that decision. Thank you."

You'll see in Attention Works on page 97 that reinforcing feedback and appreciations are far superior to change-focused feedback. In addition, reinforcing feedback and appreciations build trust, engagement, and loyalty.

4.3 Practice Effective Feedback

Offer feedback about the person's work or working relationships—specific results or behaviors. Offer other feedback at your peril.

I recommend you avoid offering feedback in these areas unless, for some reason, they affect the person's work or work relationships:

- A person's clothing or appearance. Even if you want to compliment someone, be wary of offering feedback that sounds sexist or sounds as if you are harassing the person.
- Religion: their observance or choice. Don't even go there.
- Children: how they raise children, whether they have any, all of it.
- Their significant other or any other romantic interest.

When it comes to appearance, your organization might have policies about what to wear for either safety or customer reasons.

I've offered feedback when women wore open-toed shoes in a location where that was dangerous. The environment was a prototype factory floor. We all needed closed-toe shoes. That was about physical safety.

I've offered feedback when men were too casual—the clients and customers who walked through the organization expected people to have non-holey pants and t-shirts without expletives. That was about customer expectations.

And, I once had to offer feedback when a woman's blouse gaped too low. She was unaware that other people on her team felt uncomfortable and distracted. That was about psychological safety.

People can't "just know." Someone needs to tell people.

4.3.1 Offer All Feedback in Private

I recommend you offer all feedback in private. It doesn't matter if the feedback is change-focused or reinforcing feedback. Take the time to create a private opportunity for feedback.

Why? You don't know how the person will react.

Early in my management career, I offered reinforcing feedback to someone in public. She blushed furiously, and said, "Oh, it's nothing."

I said, "It wasn't nothing to me."

I saw tears well up in her eyes and I realized I'd overstepped. She had extended herself not just intellectually, but emotionally. She was happy I had recognized her contributions. And, she was quite uncomfortable with public recognition.

Public Recognition Can Cause Problems

We hear this phrase a lot, "Praise in public. Criticize in private." That's wrong for many people.

As you can see from my mistake, this person was not comfortable with the "praise" part. She would have enjoyed my acknowledgment much more in a private setting.

Offer all feedback in private. If you want to offer public feedback afterward, ask the person if that's okay to do.

Offer feedback in private first. If you want to recognize someone in public, ask the person first. You might want to offer appreciations in private, too.

4.3.2 Use Peer-to-Peer Feedback

Managers are "higher" in the hierarchy of the organization. Sometimes, managers act more like parents or teachers when they offer feedback.

Instead, reframe your position to be that of a peer. If you think of yourself as a peer, you'll be able to offer more effective feedback. And, you'll be able to practice this feedback framework with the people you serve.

Now that you know the feedback is about the work or the work relationships, here is the feedback approach from *Behind Closed Doors: Secrets of Great Management* [BCD05]:

- Create an opening to deliver feedback.
- Describe the behavior or result in a way that the person can hear.
- State the impact on you, using "I" language.
- Make a request for changed or continued behavior.

You can use this form of feedback for either change-focused feedback or reinforcing feedback.

4.3.3 *Create an Opening for Feedback*

If you have quick feedback, you might say, leaving a meeting, "Got a couple of minutes for me to go over something with you?" If the person has another meeting, ask, "When is a good time? I think we need about ten minutes, maybe less."

If you've offered feedback about this topic before and you want more time, schedule some time with the person as soon as possible. Do not delay the feedback to a one-on-one. Especially if you only have one-on-ones every two weeks. Make time to talk to the person as soon as possible.

4.3.4 *Describe Behavior with Specific Examples*

You can't offer feedback on something you didn't observe. If someone you serve asks you to offer feedback on something they observed, try to coach that person to offer feedback themselves. Otherwise, you triangulate, and that rarely works to anyone's satisfaction.

That means the person who offers feedback needs to gather specific examples of observed behavior or results.

If you see Lucy pressure Peter for a changed estimate, you can say to Lucy, "I saw you ask Peter to reduce his estimate. To me, that looks like pressure. Can you tell me what you were thinking?"

Notice that you didn't say, "You always pressure Peter." The words "always" and "pressure" are your interpretations. If you then ask about the other person's thought process, you might learn something important.

Avoid judgments or labels such as "lazy," "always," and "never." "Lazy" is your interpretation of the person's actions. And, absolutes, such as always or never, only need one counter-example and then your feedback is useless.

4.3.5 *Explain the Impact on Your Work*

Let's say that Lucy responds in this way to your question about what she was thinking: "Every time Peter estimates something, he's always done much earlier. He doesn't pick up the next item on the board. Instead, he does all kinds of extra work that we don't need now and probably won't need later."

That's important information. It means that Lucy might not know how to offer feedback to Peter. She might have already offered feedback 57 times. You would proceed differently with either of those possibilities.

For the first option of not knowing how to offer feedback, you might say this to Lucy: "Oh, you can actually say to Peter in the moment, 'I'm not trying to pressure you. I have seen you spend a lot more time than anyone expected last week on your work, gold-plating and adding more work to the item than we, the team, thought was necessary. When you do that, I can't tell where we are for this week, and for the product as a whole.' Does that make sense to you?"

Once Lucy understands how to offer feedback to Peter, you can continue this way: "When you don't offer feedback when someone affects the entire team, I'll have trouble understanding the real state of the project. Since I report to the Ops Committee, that makes my job much more difficult."

If Lucy has offered feedback 57 times, you might say, "Wow, I hadn't realized that. Let me help you fix this problem, okay? I'm worried that the team doesn't realize you're not pressuring him. You're trying to help him work right."

If Lucy responds with, "I thought you wanted this project done faster," you can say, "Well, I do. Managers always do. But, I want the project done right, not just fast. My experience is that if we put pressure on people externally, they will cut corners. I'll start to get phone calls from various customers and that will make my job much more difficult."

Explain how this data makes your job more difficult.

4.3.6 Request What You Want

Determine the outcome you desire. Sometimes you want some joint problem-solving. Sometimes, you want to explain a narrow band of acceptable behavior.

If you desire a specific action or result, say so. If you're open to a range of possible solutions, engage in joint problem-solving.

If Peter spends too much time, you might want Lucy to offer feedback to Peter. You might even ask her to practice with you.

If Lucy has already offered feedback, you might want to her to formally escalate the problem to you to solve.

If Lucy thought you wanted the project done faster, you might want to discuss how she would know that.

As part of requesting what you want, decide how you'll follow up with each other. Reinforcing feedback doesn't often require a follow-up.

However, most change-focused feedback requires action items of some sort. Organize those and help the other person fix this problem.

4.4 People Need Transparency

People do need to know your perception of their work. Don't surprise people with feedback—that's incongruent and disrespectful. When people hear feedback that surprises them, they might wonder what else you "blame" them for, or what else you're keeping a secret.

You might not directly see the work of the people you serve. In that case, you might need to offer feedback and coaching to the people who do see their colleagues' work. I call this "meta" feedback— feedback about the feedback.

Consider reading or reviewing these books if you want more depth in your approach to feedback:

- *Behind Closed Doors: Secrets of Great Management* [BCD05], the book I wrote with Esther Derby.
- I also recommend *What Did You Say? The Art of Giving and Receiving Feedback* [SSW97] as a gentle introduction to feedback.
- I find David Rock's SCARF model helpful when I want to think about when and how to offer feedback. See the article, "SCARF: A brain-based model for collaborating with and influencing others" [ROC08].
- You might also like *Radical Candor: Be a Kick-Ass Boss Without Losing Your Humanity* [SCO17] to make sure you don't fall into any feedback traps.

As a leader, help everyone learn how to offer and receive feedback. The more often people receive and offer feedback, the more they will Create a Culture of Psychological Safety on page 6. Safety arises from a culture where people are not afraid to offer and receive helpful feedback.

Don't surprise people with feedback. Offer feedback more often, rather than less often. That works especially well if you find something to appreciate about people.

4.5 Options to Start Effective Feedback

When I work with managers, they often ask me how to start with feedback. They've never seen great feedback. Or, they've experienced the feedback "sandwich:" reinforcing feedback, then change-focused feedback, then reinforcing feedback.

If you receive the feedback sandwich, what do you hear? You might hear the first reinforcing feedback. Then you hear the change-focused feedback. Do you hear the last thing the person says?

Probably not.

And, this practice sets the other person up to expect "bad news" after something you say that you liked about their work. Practice the sandwich too much and people never hear anything that worked about their work.

If you have a lot of feedback to offer, first start with reinforcing feedback. Do you even need to offer change-focused feedback? If so, separate that feedback from the reinforcing feedback.

Remember one thing about feedback: As a society, we don't tell people often enough what we like about what they do. That's why the first two options below are about appreciations or reinforcing feedback.

Here are some possibilities for how you might start with feedback:

- Find something small if you don't think there's something big: "I appreciate you for showing that we can start and end meetings on time."
- Find something to appreciate or reinforce every day about each person on your team. Here's an example: "Thanks for facilitating that meeting this morning. I didn't realize some people weren't with me. You helped make that meeting successful."
- If you do need to offer change-focused feedback, gather the data first and make sure the person agrees with the data. You can always ask for changed behavior another time.

- Consider writing a script, especially if you're nervous. Please don't read the script. Practice from the script and then stay in the moment to react to the other person.
- Consider practicing with your manager. He or she might not realize the challenges you have.

You can always create and lead a feedback lab as part of your group's learning time. You might be able to use the lab to model appreciations.

CHAPTER 5

Is Measuring Time Useful?

Here's a problem most modern managers encounter: the organization changes the products and services the organization wants to offer. That requires the people doing the work change how they work and the tools they use. Where does that leave managers, especially if they no longer work in the work itself?

The managers don't know the details of what people do all day.

When we don't know, we create stories in our heads. And, we tend to measure the outputs, not outcomes. Those outputs are often time-based:

- Time spent at work
- Time in meetings
- Time spent updating the ticket system or the board

None of these measures have any impact on the customers. And, when we measure time, we too often make people feel as if they have to account for their time. People spend time on accounting (updating boards, spreadsheets, timesheets), not on the work.

If you no longer know how people create or test or service the product, how can you assess a person's value? This brings us back to Theory X vs. Theory Y management assumptions.

- If you want to Encourage Flow Efficiency on page 2, it doesn't matter how much any one person works. It matters if the team members can also offer and receive feedback and coaching. You might have to help people learn how to Practice Effective Feedback on page 47.

- People who don't have time to think, don't learn or experiment. They don't feel safe enough to take the time to change anything.
- If you Extend Trust on page 8 and measure outcomes, you don't need to know when people work.

Managers who attempt to manage by assessing how much time people spend become incongruent, in at least these ways:

1. Blaming the people for not spending the time the way they, the manager, would.
2. Placating the manager's manager by measuring irrelevant information.

Worse, some managers want to measure what people do by creating mandatory meetings and then assessing the time people spend in meetings.

Should you ever measure the time people spend on work? My reviewers suggested these two examples of when managers should measure the time spent:

1. When you have a customer contract where time spent is part of the contract. Andrea Goulet, of Corgibytes said, "Our clients read the time reports. It's not something that we're just doing to micromanage. It's a communication tool. Also, we use it as a way to make sure we can build in as much scheduling flexibility and autonomy as possible. We also strongly encourage people to work no more than 40 hours per week. When we didn't track time, many folks would work and not stop. We knew it was happening but didn't have data. Lastly, and this was a big insight for us, it's not just keyboard time that's billable—thinking time is tracked, too."
2. If you want to change estimate modes, such as moving from relative sizing to cycle time, you might need to measure the actuals against the estimates.

I couldn't think of a third example. You might have another example of a time when you measured the time people spent—and the people you served still trusted you.

In my experience, when managers measure time *at* work, they use that measure as a surrogate for understanding and finding ways to measure the *results* of the work. These managers measure the outputs (time spent) instead of outcomes (finished products or services).

5.1 Myth: I Can Measure the Work by Where People Spend Time

Gabe and Cynthia walked to the cafeteria together.

"Have you heard the new thing that Andrew is doing?" Gabe asked, shaking his head.

"What now?" Cynthia asked.

"We have to fill out time cards with our actual time on them. Andrew wants to know how much time we spend at work. The more time, the better."

Cynthia stopped. "Are you serious? What's he going to do with that information?"

Gabe said, "He's going to see who the 'star' players are."

Cynthia sighed. "I thought I'd seen everything, but this takes the cake. We work as teams. Why would he do this?"

"Yeah. I think he's feeling pressure from his management," Gabe said. "Hey, what if we explain we're supposed to be about 'sustainable pace.' This crazy time card thing is going to make the pace anything but sustainable—especially if he wants more hours. I don't understand why he thinks he can measure our output by the time we spend here. I have good days and bad days. Sometimes, I think I spend a lot less time here on the good days and produce twice as much! Sometimes, I stop writing code on the bad days, so I don't create four times as many bugs!"

Cynthia grinned. "Well, I've certainly had those days. How can we make Andrew see the error of his ways? Maybe get Tina, the other director, to talk to him?"

"Maybe. Or maybe we should explain that our progress doesn't have much to do with the time we spend at work. Maybe we should baseline our features per week now and measure our features per week after he does this time card thing, especially if he insists on overtime. What we have to do is make our pain his, because this is total craziness."

5.2 Time Is Not Results

I've seen managers try to reward employees by the number of hours that the employees' cars were in the parking lot. People can game that measurement easily—leave the car in the parking lot for the week.

One colleague gamed the system that way— until the snowplow plowed around his car after a surprise snowstorm. He had already gone home for the storm and had left the car. His management was quite surprised and quite angry about the employee's deception.

When you use time as a measurement for how good people's work is, you beg them to game the system and exhibit some of this crazy behavior. Time at work does not equate to good work. It never has, and it never will. Oh, you can't work without spending time working somewhere and on the work itself, but that doesn't mean that you have to spend lots of extra time at work.

5.3 How Many Hours in a Day?

Everyone's day will be different, but there is some reasonable upper limit to how much people can work in a day. People can work up to about eight good hours a day on an intellectually challenging job before mental exhaustion sets in.

Some people might be useful and work for fewer than eight hours. If the team members pair or mob on the work, they might only be able to work about six hours together before they exhaust their ability to think.

Long hours don't mean that people produce more. (See "The Research is Clear: Long Hours Backfire for People and Companies."[1]) Some results of long hours:

- We make mistakes because we are tired.
- We live in higher stress, which results in health problems. That might increase the organization's insurance costs.
- The more tired and stressed we feel, the more likely we are to miss work or even leave because of the job. Replacing a knowledge worker might cost two or three times their salary.

If you want people to accomplish more work, then restrict their work time to no more than eight hours a day. That includes weekends and evenings.

You might be wondering, "Huh? Restrict the time at work?" Yes. You may have heard of Parkinson's Law, "Work expands to fill the time allotted."

When you restrict work time, people focus and tend to collaborate. (Unless you've created draconian personal objectives.) Their throughput increases because their focus and collaboration increases.

5.4 Manage the Work in Progress

When you timebox the time people spend at work, they start to make decisions about their work:

- People postpone the not-important-enough-yet work.
- They begin to say "no" to more work.
- They rank the remaining work.

---

[1] https://hbr.org/2015/08/the-research-is-clear-long-hours-backfire-for-people-and-for-companies

They start to manage their WIP (Work in Progress). And, with any luck, they work in flow efficiency to finish more work as a team. (See Encourage Flow Efficiency on page 2.)

People are smart. They will decide to *complete* the most essential work. If they are not sure, they will ask you. Expect some tough questions about which projects/work are most important. That's okay because if you are a manager, you need to be able to answer those difficult questions.

Remember, people are not machines. If you don't rank the work in a project portfolio, they will decide which work they will do and when.

5.5 Which Meetings Can We Kill?

Once you manage the project portfolio and flow work through the ranked projects with teams, it's time to review the time people spend in meetings.

If you decide that you only have eight hours to work, one thing you must do is make decisions about meetings. Do you need to attend those meetings? Maybe not. Maybe someone else can go for you. Is that meeting essential for anyone?

If a meeting is essential, it will have an agenda—that the meeting facilitator sent in advance. It will have minutes. It will have a list of action items, and someone will manage them so that people are accountable for their action items.

If you attend meetings where there are no agendas, minutes, or action items, maybe you don't have to attend. Now, don't just drop the meeting on the floor. That's rude.

However, if you tell the meeting leader that unless you see an agenda, minutes, and action items for the meeting, you will not be participating in future meetings, then you have provided enough notice to stop your participation. And, you have provided an out for the meeting leader, too.

You might want to add a measurement called the Return On Time Invested to the end of every meeting. (See *Behind Closed Doors:*

Secrets of Great Management [BCD05] and *Create Your Successful Agile Project: Collaborate, Measure, Estimate, Deliver* [ROT17] for more details.)

Use this five-point scale to ask people to report how much value they received for the time they invested in the meeting.

ROTI Ratings

0: No benefit received for time invested.
1: A little better than 0. Some benefit, but not commensurate with time invested.
2: Value received equal to time invested.
3: A little better than even return.
4: High benefit. Value received greater than time invested.

Figure 5.1: ROTI Ratings

The meeting leader or facilitator can ask people to create a histogram of the meeting's value to each person, as in this image:

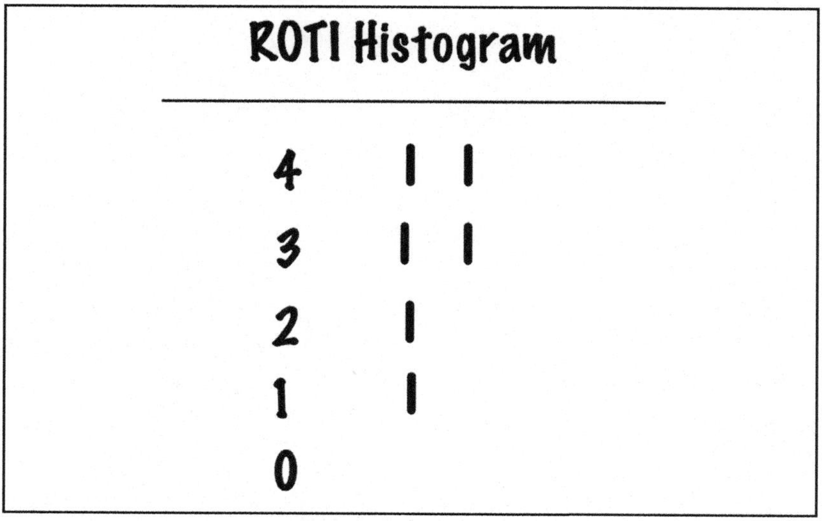

ROTI Histogram

4   I I
3   I I
2   I
1   I
0

Figure 5.2: ROTI Histogram

In this example, I would ask the people who labeled the meeting a 2 or 1 for more information. Maybe I didn't run the meeting well. Maybe we needed some preparation time. Maybe they weren't the right people to participate.

Meetings can offer value. You might find that you can exercise leadership by helping to change your organization's meeting culture.

Once you address meeting time, you might realize that people—including you—might need to reorganize their days.

5.6 What Does Your Day Look Like?

As with meetings, email might not be the first thing people think of when you tell them to timebox their days.

I find that I have about three chunks of time that I can work in a day: a two-hour piece in the morning and two other two-hour chunks in the afternoon. That adds up to six hours of work in a day. When I ask colleagues and clients about their days, they often tell me they have fewer chunks of work time in their days. The more senior the manager, the fewer large chunks of time, because the manager tends to have more meetings and interruptions. Your mileage and workday will vary.

Technical people might choose to finish work in their significant chunks of work time, rather than spend that time on email or chat. Encourage behavior that helps a person or a team finish customer-valuable work, rather than on email or chat.

Of course, the more geographically distributed the team is, the more email or chat is a part of the team's work. That's unfortunate because there is plenty of other emails that are *not* part of a technical person's work that arrives in an inbox. The more email a person has to process, the less time for technical work. The longer a person can go between processing emails, the more technical work a person can do. It is that simple.

One of the most productive things you can do for email processing is to turn off any signals that tell you that more email has arrived.

Assume you have more email. It's a reasonable assumption. Then, decide how many times a day you can safely process email.

When I explain this trick to my coaching clients, there is always a pregnant pause. "But, I'm supposed to answer email within five minutes of receiving it!"

If people want you to answer a question right away, then they should pick up the phone or text you. Email is for low-bandwidth communication—a fact that runs counter to too many corporate cultures.

5.7 When Do You Need to Respond?

Does your device give you an audible notification for every email, call, or text? Many of my clients tell me they are at the mercy of their phones.

Managers often feel the need to respond right away. Worse, they might then interrupt a technical person or a team if the manager needs an answer.

Back in Decide When to Conduct One-on-Ones on page 38 I discussed the cost of an interruption to a technical person and a manager. Everyone deserves time to think.

See if you can create working agreements across the organization about when to use email, text, or calls. How will you agree—as an organization—about when to use synchronous and asynchronous communication? Not everything deserves to interrupt you. Not every request needs an immediate response.

You might need to set guardrails for yourself, if not the organization, about when people should expect a response to the various ways of contacting you.

5.8 Measure Results, Not Time

Knowledge workers work at different paces on different days. The way to help people work faster is to encourage them to work together (pairing, swarming, or mobbing) on small requirements.

Instead of time, think about the results you want. I find that I want to see these kinds of results or outcomes:

- A demonstration that shows how we increased our knowledge of the problem.
- A demonstration or other results that help us learn more about our risks.
- A demonstration that offers us feedback about the product.

Each of these outcomes reflects what the customers buy—that's what we pay people to do. And, when a team works in flow efficiency, they can create these demonstrations faster.

You pay your software people for completed features. If you want more features, make sure they work absolutely no more than forty hours per week. Fewer hours may help people be more productive. Working more hours per week is guaranteed to get you worse results.

That's why working in flow efficiency makes so much sense instead of resource efficiency.

5.9 Create Experiments to See Where People Spend Time

Too often, I discover that what my gut thinks is true about the organization is false. The way I discover this is with data.

When I've run these experiments, the results surprised people in the past. The first experiment was creating a value stream map to label the valuable work and not-valuable work.

5.9.1 *Assess the Value Stream Map*

I once consulted with an organization that required signoffs from managers when a team completed their work. I created a value stream map so they could see when the team completed their work and the additional time needed for the signoff work.

When I showed them that the time required for signoff was *as long* as the time the team took to finish their work, the managers were surprised. We discussed the problems the managers wanted to solve. They decided they could specify the outcomes the managers wanted, and the constraints, and let the team decide how to achieve those outcomes inside the constraints.

See examples of a value stream map in Help the Team Measure Their Cycle Time on page 159.

You might need the value stream map for the next experiment, which is to assess the activities that add value, to achieve the outcomes.

5.9.2 Assess the Value-Add Activities

The second experiment is assessing the various activities and how they add value to the product.

For product development teams, these activities add value to the product itself:

- Adding a feature.
- Fixing a problem in the product.
- Discussing what problems a proposed feature solves.
- Creating automated tests so the team can easily change or fix the product.

For support teams, the value-add activities might be:

- Real-time calls with a customer.
- Resolving a customer's problem.
- Gathering feedback from a customer.

Technical Excellence Adds to Product Value

I still hear about organizational leaders who tell a team to stop writing various tests. Their reason? "We don't have time for testing."

Tests, reviews, spikes, and other interim product assessments add to the product value. That's because they add to what we know about the product. Automated tests at all levels help us see quickly what's working and what's not working. And, if we create errors, we have the supporting infrastructure to fix that problem.

To deliver fast, to add value to the product, maintain technical excellence. Those activities add significant value to the product.

Some activities do *not* add value to the product, even while they might add value to our work lives:

- Team learning meetings.
- One-on-one meetings.
- Breaks, such as a coffee break or a bio-break.

Now, consider these activities:

- Any status meeting.
- Any estimation meeting if the managers plan to change the estimate later.
- Any meeting that does not have an agenda and outcomes.

Sometimes, I ask teams to assess the ratio of value-add to non-value-add activities. Sometimes, I ask managers to assess their activities.

The more meetings we have, the less time people spend in value-add activities. When I see teams and managers spend 50% or more of their time in non-value-add activities, I realize we have a meeting-happy culture.

We will still have some non-value-add activities. However, the more we Encourage Flow Efficiency on page 2, the more time we spend in value-add activities.

The third experiment was the number of hours per week experiment.

5.10 Experiment with the Number of Hours per Week

People who work long hours think they also work hard. They are. But they are often not working smart. If you have a lot to do, I find it easier to work smart, not just hard and long.

I've worked with several managers who believed in the illusion that work-time had some sort of correspondence to the organization's throughput. I've also worked with teams who thought overtime was fine because *they* chose it.

Here's an experiment I used many times to help see what was going on. We agreed on these results:

- We could measure completed features and the cycle time for the completion. That way, we had a count of what we completed and could calculate the average time it took us.
- We also measured the Fault Feedback Ratio (FFR), the number of bad fixes to the total number of fixes.

The experiment itself was in several parts:

5.10.1 Part A: 40 Hours/Week

1. We decided on a duration of two weeks of 40 hours each week. Everyone committed to working no more than 40 hours in either of the weeks. Teams policed themselves.
2. Count the number of features the team completes and calculate the cycle time to complete each feature. Measure the Fault Feedback Ratio. If you can, also measure the cumulative flow to see where the work is. (See *Create Your Successful Agile Project* [ROT17] for these and other possible data.)

Now, we had "normal" week data.

5.10.2 Part B: 50 Hours/Week

The next two weeks:

1. Decide on the number of hours you want the team, or the team decides to work. My teams often chose 50 hours. A few teams chose 60 hours. The teams policed themselves.
2. For each week, use the same measures as above: Number of completed features, cycle time, FFR, and cumulative flow.

Now, we have overtime week data.

5.10.3 Part C: 40 Hours/Week

Now, what happens if you return to normal weeks? I often discover that people are still tired from the overtime weeks. They persist in creating more defects and incomplete work. Measure this for another two weeks:

1. Run two weeks of 40 hours each week. Everyone puts in 40 hours.
2. Report on how easy/difficult it is for each person to return to a 40-hour week.
3. For each week, use the same measures as above: Number of completed features, cycle time, FFR, and cumulative flow.

I once tried to repeat the experiment with a 30-hour week, but no one left at the six-hour mark each day. No one in the team nor I could leave at the end of just six hours. The experiment failed.

We all met during the second day, had a big laugh, and said, "Can we do 35 hours this week?" Some of us were better at leaving after seven hours of work every day. We were not perfect at it. We continued to count the same data.

5.10.4 Part D: Compare Data

Now, compare your results, recognizing that Fault Feedback Ratio is a lagging indicator, especially if you work in two-week iterations.

Some questions to ask the team:

- Did we actually complete more features when we worked overtime?

- Did we create problems for ourselves because our FFR was high?
- What was our WIP, and did that change if we worked more hours or fewer?
- How did we feel when we worked 40 hours? When we worked 50 hours?
- How easy was it to return to 40 hours? Or change to any other time.

Your team might have other questions or results they don't expect. Explore that data. Your data is superior to your gut and will offer you evidence for how to be most productive at work.

5.11 Measure Outcomes Instead of Time

Remember that our brains get tired. Even if we move around and provide our brains oxygen, water, and a little food now and then, it's not enough. Our brains need a break.

I bet you've also had excellent ideas in the shower, in your dreams, while talking with others, while *not* working. When our subconscious brain works, we might have breakthrough ideas.

Don't just work long. Work smart.

5.12 Manage Your Timesheet Time

As an engineer, I had to submit my timesheet on Friday at noon. Yes, before the end of the day. I was supposed to account for all the time I spent on all the various projects and in what form I spent my time. Design, coding, support—they all had different codes.

And, I was only supposed to put 40 hours on my timesheet. That experience taught me several things:

- The timesheet data was hopelessly inaccurate if I worked on more than one project at a time. Even if I tried to fill out the timesheet each day, I didn't remember where I spent my time.

- After a while, the Finance people pressured me to move to a new phase of the project, so they could capitalize the project's expenses.
- If I was only supposed to report 40 hours, I only worked 40 hours.

Your managers might ask for this information. Do what you need to do. However, I would focus on asking a team to work in flow efficiency before asking them to fill out timesheets. If everyone works together on the same project, you can fill out a timesheet for the entire team. And, the accounting will be accurate.

And, if you, as the manager, are supposed to break all your work into many buckets for the Finance people, consider asking what they want the data for. What decisions will they make based on this data? You might be able to offer a different frame that satisfies their needs.

Some agencies have client contracts that require a project accounting. In that case, do comply with the accounting. And, help the client realize that the time people spend on the project accounting is time the people aren't delivering results.

See if you can measure outcomes or results: what customers can use or buy.

5.13 Options For Measuring Outcomes or Results

The first question I ask is this: How will we know our work achieved the results we want? You have at least these options:

1. Start with the project or group goal and work up to more organizational results.
2. Define the outcomes you want the team to achieve. Sometimes, the team needs to explore the problem first. Then, you and the team can jointly define the outcomes.
3. While I no longer recommend OKRs for my clients, you might find them useful. Consider using OKRs (Objectives, and Key Results), and determine measures as you work down to product

or service objectives with the relevant measures. (I'll discuss more about OKRs in Book 3, but you might like these references to start: *Measure What Matters: How Google, Bono, and the Gates Foundation Rock the World with OKRs* [DOE18] and *Radical Focus: Achieving Your Most Important Goals with Objectives and Key Results* [WOD16]). In my experience, too many of my clients create objectives that are outputs.

4. At a minimum, consider an impact map for the product or service you're working on, and generate the results you want. You might have to work backward from the usual way you would create a map. See *Impact Mapping: Making a big impact with software products and projects* [ADZ12] for more details.

Never measure an individual's work. Measuring an individual does not Encourage Flow Efficiency on page 2.

If you worry about whether people are as effective as they can be at work, consider these measures:

- Organizational lead time: How long does it take the organization, from the time someone has an idea until the customer can use that idea as a product or service?

- Organizational cycle time: How long does it take the organization, from the time one team has the idea on its backlog to deliver that item as a product or service?

- Organizational time to discover and fix customer-affecting defects or problems: How long does it take the organization to restore a customer's ability to work?

I'll explain more about these measurements in Visualize the System on page 158.

In my experience, the managers spend more time deciding than teams spend working. I hope I'm wrong about your organization.

CHAPTER 6

How Can You Tell if People Are Engaged?

A senior manager watched people leave at 5:30 P.M. He became frustrated. He said, "I want people to show me they're invested and motivated to do a great job." He equated that with people working overtime.

I asked him why he thought people lacked investment or motivation. He said, "I know by the hours they work. I work plenty of hours."

I wanted to explain that working too many hours wasn't smart or necessary. This manager thought that seeing the time people worked was useful. (See Is Measuring Time Useful? on page 55.)

Instead of time, I asked him what *outcomes* he would see if people were motivated. We agreed on finished features, projects that ended, and satisfied customers as a start.

We discussed the difference between management work and the time that takes versus technical work and the time it requires. We discussed the fact that in-depth thinking takes lots of brainpower and that people get tired at the end of a good day of work.

At that point, he yawned. I suggested he might have already put in a good day of work. Maybe we could connect in the morning instead of working past a reasonable hour.

This manager was not stupid—not at all. He had forgotten how management work is different from technical work:

- Managers multitask by design. As managers work through problems, they realize they need more information or more or different people to make a decision.
- Managers, especially senior managers, often have bonuses that create different incentives than the knowledge workers do. For example, if your bonus is in stock, you might make short-term decisions to drive up the stock price.

And, because we are all people, some of the same rules apply. Tell people the results you want. Ask them to collaborate on the problem with their peers. Give them any tools they need. Then, give them the autonomy to do their jobs. You're much more likely to get the results you want.

Money is not sufficient for employee engagement. And you can't tell if people are engaged or invested in your company by seeing their work hours.

6.1 Myth: I Need to Know People Are Invested

Dave, the CIO, strode down the hall to see Sarah, the delivery services manager. He walked in, carefully closed the door, and sat down.

"Sarah, we need to talk. I don't like the ship you're running here. Everyone leaves between 5 P.M. and 5:30 P.M. They walk out! How can you expect to get through everything we need to get done this quarter? They're not invested! They're not engaged!"

Sarah carefully saved what she was doing and turned to her boss. "Dave, is there a problem with our deliveries? Are we not delivering what we said we would? As far as I know, we've delivered everything we committed to. I know you want more than we can do. I understand you want more, and we are working on seeing what we can do. But we are delivering what we commit to. What's the real problem?"

Dave exploded and jumped up to pace, "People leave! At five o'clock! Don't they know we need commitment? We need everyone rowing the same boat here!"

Sarah was confused by the ship references. "Dave, what is this with the boat and ship business? What have you seen or heard that makes you believe we are not committed or engaged?"

Dave continued to pace. "How can you think they're all committed and engaged when they leave so early?"

"They're not leaving early," she said.

Dave started to open his mouth.

"No, you barged in here," she said. "Let me talk now. The teams work together as cross-functional teams. Everyone arrives before 9 a.m. so they can start their day as a team. Some teams do standups. Some start off mobbing. They work all day as a team. By 5 P.M., they're tired. By 5:30 P.M., they are more than done. Do you want tired people working on your codebase or tests or documentation? No, you do not. You want people who have put in an honest day of work, and that's it. You don't need people to work overtime."

Dave sat there, shaking his head. "But what if they get great ideas at home?"

Sarah continued. "I've told them to take index cards home. If they have a good idea or a great idea, they can write it down on an index card. That way, they don't lose it. The next day, they bring the index card back to work, and then they can implement their great idea."

"Index cards instead of code or tests when they're home???" Dave's face got red.

"Hang on," Sarah said. "We measured the results of this. Our defect counts have gone way down. Our innovation, our new ideas, have gone way up. Why? Because people are not overtired. They are happy with their families or their social lives. They are healthy because they are eating properly and going to the gym. Now, what is the problem, exactly?"

"I need you to finish more projects. I also need to know people are engaged."

"Look, the engagement will come from how they work and their ability to finish their work. And, if you want more work done, you have two choices. You can take projects off our portfolio so we can focus on less at a time or let me hire more people. But you can't just get more work out of the people we have. People can't think *more*. Or harder. Or faster. Or whatever cliché you want to use. If you like, we can brainstorm more ideas on how to get more projects done. But don't tell me to have people work overtime. That's crazy. I won't do it."

Dave sighed and shook his head. "I just don't know."

"All these people are engaged," Sarah said. "They're invested in our customers. What more could you want?"

6.2 Management Work is Different From Technical Work

A manager's day is fraught with interruption and context switching at least every hour, if not more often. Many managers feel as if they need to wait until 5 P.M. to get anything done. They might.

Too many managers have forgotten or never known how a great technical day feels. When professional people focus and deliver, they concentrate on their work for significant periods. And, if the team is part of an agile team, they might swarm, pair, or mob, using even more concentration.

When managers ask people to work overtime, they are not thinking about how technical people need to focus during the day. They don't realize what focused teams do.

Let's imagine you're a technical person who has arranged your day so that you have a two-hour chunk in the morning and a couple more two-hour chunks in the afternoon. You might work alone or as part of a team in these chunks. However, if you have worked hard and finished deliverables, you have accomplished your work for the day.

Your brain is now tired, and you need to leave. And, if you're like me, if you collaborate a lot, you become quite tired. (I find the real-time collaboration more tiring because I have to talk and think out loud. Even as an extrovert, thinking and working out loud tires me out. I need to stop to refresh my brain for the next day.

If you are not lucky enough to have several chunks of concentration-time, you context switch all day. The more you context switch, the more exhausted you are. (The less effective, too.) You need to leave at the end of the day and understand how to organize your next day, so you accomplish more.

The difference between management work is just one piece of this engagement/invested puzzle. The other part is about trust.

6.3 I'm Invested, Why Aren't They?

Many managers think that when people work long hours, those people are invested or engaged in the organization. That's not true. People work long hours for many reasons—most of them based on fear. You can't tell if people are invested or engaged by the hours they work.

One senior executive asked me this question, "I'm invested. Why aren't the people in my organization as invested as I am?"

I asked him if he used open-book management. Did people know the purpose of all the projects and where the money went?

"No."

I asked him if he shared all the profits equally. He looked horrified. "No, of course not. I started this company. I should own more of it. I deserve the sweat equity."

I asked him why he thought everyone should be as invested as he was. He didn't share the purpose of the organization. And, he kept the lion's share of the profits. Why did he think everyone would be as invested as he was?

After that conversation, the executive walked away, concerned. How could he reward people and get the results he wanted?

He was going to have to change the way he thought about investing in people. Not expect that people were invested or engaged with the time they worked.

That senior manager had a huge problem: he didn't extend trust.

Knowledge workers don't work *primarily* for money. As Dan Pink explained in *Drive: The Surprising Truth About What Motivates Us* [PIN11], as long as the company pays you *enough* money, you work for autonomy, mastery, and purpose.

When you have all three, you also gain the respect and trust of the people with whom you work. In addition, the people become a symmathesy, the product of their joint learning, as in Nora Bateman's essay, *Symmathesy: A Word in Progress* [BAT15].

When senior managers look for time and not results as a way of engagement, they miss the point. They miss opportunities to engage people in a cause larger than themselves.

People engage in their work when management trusts them enough to jointly create an environment of autonomy, mastery, and purpose.

6.4 **What's the Real Problem?**

Many managers want people to have the same sense of investment in the organization as the manager does. In that case, you might find it useful to ask these questions:

- How much autonomy do people have, especially around how they do their work?
- Do they understand why they are doing this work?
- Do people feel a sense of mastery about their work?

You might need to know the answer to this question also:

Do I know what people want from their careers, to be engaged?

People may understand their purpose. They might have a chance to master their craft. They might feel autonomous. And, they might be snowed under with too much work, especially if the organization assumes people are resources and manages and measures people that way, where they do *not* Encourage Flow Efficiency on page 2.

What About Engagement Surveys?

I have not found engagement surveys to be useful enough to justify the time and expense of doing them. You might have other data.

If you conduct one-on-ones and build a relationship with each person you serve, you don't need engagement surveys.

Sometimes, managers think they can measure people by the time they spend at work. (See Is Measuring Time Useful? on page 55.)

Wanting people to work overtime is related to that myth. When you force people to timebox their work to just an eight-hour workday, they start making choices about the work they do and don't do. They stop doing time-wasting work. They start doing useful work, and they start collaborating. But, only if you stop interfering.

Remember, only adults work in your organization. If you want different results, look at the environment you have created. Does it allow for autonomy, mastery, and purpose? If not, what do you need to do?

6.5 Options to Increase Engagement

I like to think about purpose, mastery, autonomy, and safety as ways to increase engagement.

1. Purpose: Have you or your managers articulated the purpose of the team's and organization's work? Making money is not a purpose. Making money is an outcome of people delivering to a specific purpose. When people know the problems they solve for particular customers, they engage in the work.
2. Mastery: People feel as if they are part of some team so that they can learn together. That increases their mastery.
3. Autonomy: People have the ability—within the corporate guardrails—to create a work environment that encourages

personal or team autonomy so the people can decide what to do. The policies support behaviors you want, rather than explicitly punishing bad behavior.

4. Safety: The team can manage their interpersonal behaviors well. They can offer each other feedback and coaching.

Your team's culture and the greater corporate culture define how well people engage. That means you can use respect as a guideline.

If you treat people with respect and use your management integrity, they are unlikely to create an unsafe environment. If you encourage discussions with respect, people are likely to discuss difficult issues with respect. And, if you reward with respect—teams or groups of people who work together to deliver the results you need—you will also maintain high employee engagement.

As soon as you lose management integrity, you're likely to lose employee engagement.

CHAPTER 7

How Do You Know People are Working Hard?

A corollary to How Can You Tell if People Are Engaged? on page 73 is this myth, the myth of whether people are working hard.

Managers have few tools to assess how hard people work. Beware of focusing on interim measures or outputs. While those things might be easy to measure, those measures are too often meaningless.

Instead, focus on outcomes. Did the team finish a feature, learn from an experiment, or solve a problem for a customer? Those are outcomes, results.

Here's the myth about thinking that knowledge work is all about typing.

7.1 Myth: If You're Not Typing, You're Not Working

"James, I need to talk to you about Bill." Suzanne shut the door and sat down in the visitor chair.

"Okay, what's up?" James stopped typing at his computer. He walked to his visitor table and sat down.

"I just walked by Bill's office. He's leaning back in his chair. I could swear he's snoring!" Suzanne yanked at her sleeves, her brow furrowed. "He's not working. If he's not typing, how could he be working?"

"Suzanne, what did you do before you were the CIO?" James decided to lead her to the answer instead of answering directly.

"What do you mean? I was a manager of technology."

"Okay, and before that?"

"I was a project manager. And a darn good one."

"I bet you were. How long has it been since you did technical work? Fifteen years? Twenty years? I'm not asking your age. I'm making a point about different personalities and technical work."

Suzanne arched one eyebrow.

"Some people need to think about their work," James said. "Sometimes, they take a walk. Sometimes, they lean back in their chairs, and they close their eyes. Sometimes, when Bill does that, he actually does nap. It's okay; it won't be for more than ten, maybe fifteen minutes. When he wakes up and opens his eyes, he's going to have a terrific idea—or, more likely, three terrific ideas—that he will share with the team."

Suzanne arched the other eyebrow.

"Some people need to discuss their work to generate ideas. If Bill were having a meeting with people, would you object?"

"No, of course not!" she said.

"Right. And if Bill had decided to make himself a cup of coffee, that would have been fine. Or if he'd gone to work out in the gym, that would have been okay. But because you happened to see him lean back in the chair with his eyes closed, it wasn't okay."

Suzanne shook her head.

James continued. "Bill thinks best by himself, but he also pairs really well with other people. He just came off several days of constant pairing. He told everyone he needed an hour off to regenerate."

Suzanne said, "Oh. I didn't realize that."

James nodded. "I didn't think so," he said. "Trish is different. She needs to take a long walk to regroup. She takes a walk around the campus to think. Danny is also different. He wants to discuss things with people. Loudly. You know when Danny's thinking. Everyone knows when Danny's thinking."

Suzanne grinned and nodded. "I certainly do. Sometimes, I think I can hear him in my office."

James laughed. "You might," he said, "The point is this: You and I can't tell when people are thinking. We have to trust that they are working, even when they're not typing. Because I'm their manager, you need to trust me. I trust them to work. Do you trust me?"

Suzanne leaned back in the chair. "Yes, I trust you. How do you know all this about your people?"

"Well, I observe them. I talk to them. Remember when you asked me to take on managing all those other people directly, and I told you I couldn't? I told you my max number of people was about two agile teams? That I had to be able to have one-on-ones with every person every other week?"

Suzanne nodded.

"This is why. I get to know people in our one-on-ones. I walk around and listen. I'm available if they need me to facilitate their problem-solving. I don't insinuate myself into the teams, but I'm there if they need me. I help people with meta-coaching and meta-feedback. I didn't learn all of this the first day I was their manager. I learned it over time, bit by bit."

"Oh," Suzanne said.

"I don't always get it right," James said. "But I don't impose on the team. I get it right more often than I get it wrong. When you came in here worried about Bill, I knew what was going on. I wasn't worried."

"So it's all about knowing your team and trusting them to do their jobs," Suzanne said. "Well, I trust you. And I guess, by extension, I trust them."

7.2 Trust People to Use Their Best Work Approach

If you ask a developer or tester what takes the most time in software product development, they often say, "thinking" or "investigation."

Both of those activities are primarily reading the code or tests or talking with people about the code or tests. Thinking and investigation might involve writing notes or drawing.

Thinking is about envisioning how the product works now or could work. People envision in any number of ways. They often don't type much when they're envisioning.

We use many activities to create a successful product.

- We might write requirements in some form, such as use cases or user stories. Agile teams often write requirements as a team.
- We might develop paper prototypes for the GUI or try some other user interface, which is not typing.
- We might create several small features so we could experiment with scaling a system in the large or the system architecture. That's a combination of generating a hypothesis or two, maybe writing a little code with the necessary tests, and then assessing the outcome of the experiments.

Some of these activities require reading the previous code or tests. Some of them require discussion with the rest of the team. And, some people might read and then write a test, read some more, write another test, and so on.

Some people prefer to work alone. Many agile teams encourage the team or parts of the team to work together. In that case, people rarely type all at the same time. However, they are working.

Typing is the least of what happens in almost any form of knowledge work. The team discusses the work. They might design by writing on a whiteboard or creating tests and code. They get feedback from each other and their interim products as they proceed.

When I ask people outside of software—for example, chemists—they describe a similar flow of work. They create hypotheses that lead to experiments. They decide what to measure. They set up the experiment and let it run until the chemists can gather the data. The chemists then think about their results.

Much of the work is thinking. Some thinking occurs with other people—and sometimes at volume. Some thinking occurs when people assess the results of their experiments. For software people, much of the thinking happens when they read the code and tests that existed before they touched this part of the product.

Software people, regardless of their specialty within the team, tend to read to understand much more than they need to type. Because teams need to learn together—and some workgroups also need to learn together—consider working as a team.

The more people collaborate in real-time, the more intense the work is. We might need a break every so often to recharge.

You might, too.

7.3 Recharge Yourself

How do you recharge yourself during the day? I make sure to drink enough and walk. Every so often, I take brief naps. You might want another way.

Even naps during the day can help us recharge. Dan Pink, in *When: The Scientific Secrets of Perfect Timing* [PIN18] explains how brief naps can help reset our brains. Sometimes, we even gain a flash of insight when we take and then wake from short naps.

Many of my manager colleagues spend all day in meetings where they can't nap, don't have easy access to water, and they don't get up and move around. Some of them don't mind the lack of water because they claim they can't take time for a bio break.

However, these people fool themselves. I have been in meetings with managers—in their 30's and 40's—who regularly fell asleep because they hadn't taken the time to recharge.

Some colleagues have a walking partner. They walk several times a day for 10-15 minutes at a time. Long enough to get their blood flowing. Not so long that they can't return to their work context.

Some of my colleagues prefer to move. They use the on-site gym. Sometimes, they play a quick game of ping-pong, foosball, or even frisbee.

If you're tired or stuck, change something about your work. Do not just sit there.

We have data that one of the worst things we can do to finish work is to sit in one chair all day long.[1] In addition to that reference, there's another study about how bad sedentary behavior is for us: Patterns of sedentary behavior and mortality in U.S. middle-aged and older adults: A national cohort study.[2]

Instead of sitting still, consider when is the right time to move.

- Use the Pomodoro Technique. Work for 25 minutes and then take a five-minute break. You must stand up and move in that five-minute break. Then, repeat after the stretching. (See *Pomodoro Technique Illustrated: The Easy Way to Do More in Less Time* [NOT10] for more details.)
- If you pair with someone, make sure you alternate position as the driver or navigator at least every fifteen to twenty minutes. I happen to prefer changing every ten minutes.
- When teams mob, they often rotate in as little as eight minutes. Yes, every eight minutes, the driver and navigators change—and in some teams—the entire team stands up and moves their chairs.

When we move, we increase our blood flow to our brains. You might gain some other side benefits, depending on how much you move. A physical activity break of five to ten minutes is good for you every hour or so. The smaller the chunk of work you have to complete, the easier this is to accomplish.

If you work at home, you might even consider a short nap—about ten to fifteen minutes' worth. Some businesses encourage

---

[1] https://www.mayoclinic.org/healthy-lifestyle/adult-health/expert-answers/sitting/faq-20058005

[2] https://www.ncbi.nlm.nih.gov/pubmed/28892811

brief naps at work,[3] but I have yet to experience an organization like that.

You might suggest these or other alternatives to people who need to recharge during the day. And, all of us do need to renew.

7.4 Extend Trust to the People Doing the Work

How do you know people aren't wasting time? Let's reason a little about knowledge work.

I cannot think of a kind of knowledge work where we don't need to learn with the rest of our team as a symmathesy. The team learns together. They learn:

- How the product is supposed to work
- How the product is supposed to act and look
- How to expose the risks as they create the product

The people who build the product learn together as they create.

What do you think when you see someone "thinking" with their eyes closed? You might agree with Suzanne above—how could that person possibly be working?

You might not realize any of these possibilities:

- People have just come off substantial team time and they're relaxing for a few minutes.
- Some people meditate for a few minutes several times during the day.
- Some people focus with their eyes closed.

Consider this: make a note of the time and ask the person later. You can extend trust and learn the context later. You might see a point in time that does not reflect the whole of a person's workday.

---

[3] https://www.nytimes.com/2017/06/23/smarter-living/take-naps-at-work-apologize-to-no-one.html

If you're anxious about people "goofing off," encourage teams to collaborate closely. The more you Encourage Flow Efficiency on page 2, the more the *team* completes work. The team knows who works and who doesn't.

7.5 Consider Team-Based Options for Work

If you encourage team-based collaboration, you never have to worry about whether people take too much time off. The team "polices" itself.

In Recharge Yourself on page 85, I suggested you encourage the team to collaborate as a team, as in pairing or mobbing. There's a third possibility: swarming.

- Pairing is when two people work on one item. They share a keyboard and a monitor. They trade off who types and who reviews as they proceed.
- Swarming is when the entire team works on one item. They each do their work, checking back in with each other regularly. I prefer a check-in every hour. At the check-in, stuck people ask for help. And, if someone is done with everything he or she could do, that person offers help to the other team members.
- Mobbing is when the entire team works on one item, with one keyboard and one (large) monitor. Only one person types at a time. The rest of the team discusses how to proceed and directs the typist. The team rotates through who types, making sure every person has a chance.

(For more information, see the post about Pairing, Swarming, and Mobbing,[4] or read *Create Your Successful Agile Project: Collaborate, Measure, Estimate, Deliver* [ROT17].)

When teams work as teams, you don't have to worry if people are working hard. They are. You don't have to worry that people waste time. They aren't.

---

[4] https://www.jrothman.com/mpd/project-management/2016/07/pairing-swarming-and-mobbing/

Teams who collaborate manage themselves and their actions better and faster than a manager can. If you trust the team to collaborate, they will work as fast as they can, because the team finds and manages its rhythm.

The real issue with flow efficiency is how to recognize and reward people. I'll address a little of that in the next myth and continue in Book 3.

CHAPTER 8

What Value do Performance Reviews Offer?

You've probably received several performance reviews in your career. Have any of those reviews:

- Created more trust and loyalty between you and your manager?
- Created more loyalty between you and your team?
- Created more loyalty between you and the organization (also known as employee engagement)?

When I ask people these questions, they often say, "NO!" and then tell me stories about how their reviews made them want to look for other jobs.

I received two performance reviews that made me trust my manager more. Maybe you have a better experience than I do.

All the other performance reviews? I trusted the managers less. I became less loyal to the manager or the organization—and more loyal to my team. The organization didn't "engage" me—the work and the team did.

I found the entire experience aggravating, irritating, and demeaning. Aggravating because even when I gave my bosses my yearly list of accomplishments, they only remembered the last three or four months' worth of time. Irritating, because most of the time, the manager hadn't prepared well. And demeaning, because the manager didn't understand enough about my contributions.

I've had a much better experience when I received feedback, not an evaluation.

I have received some helpful feedback in performance reviews. Much of that feedback was too late to make a difference during an entire year. I wrote about that in Do I Really Need to Tell Someone How They're Doing? on page 41.

I've also received feedback-in-the-moment about how I needed to let people on a project come to me with bad news. That was helpful feedback, and I didn't receive it at a performance review, thank goodness. That would have been way too late. I was able to change my behavior—then and there.

When I became a manager, I had to write performance evaluations for the people I served. I didn't like it, but I did it. I thought it was crazy because the people worked in cross-functional teams. The people on the teams knew more about what "my" people did than I did. Yes, even though I had one-on-ones. Yes, even though I asked everyone for a list of accomplishments in advance. But, it was the way it was. I thought I couldn't buck city hall.

But now, we have two ideas changing organizational culture—flow efficiency and agile approaches—have blown the idea of performance evaluations wide open. And ranking people? That never worked. I'll write about that in Book 3.

I've been a consultant for over 25 years. I have not received a formal performance review during that time. I've received plenty of feedback. Even when I haven't enjoyed the feedback, I have appreciated the fact that I received it.

Remember, I was inside organizations for almost 20 years. I received fewer than 15 performance reviews. Somehow, my bosses never quite got around to them. They hated doing them. I know that one of my bosses wrote them with the help of a glass of Scotch; he told me so.

Feedback is useful. Performance reviews? Not only aren't they useful. They're often downright harmful. I'll include references at the end.

8.1 Myth: Evaluation via Performance Reviews Are Useful

Bill popped his head into Jan's office as he was leaving for the evening.

"Jan, do you have a minute? I have to do performance reviews tonight. I was going to drink Scotch and work my way through all of them."

Jan laughed and said, "Sure. Scotch might make you feel good, but it will definitely not solve your performance review problem." She paused. "Why are you still doing performance reviews? I stopped doing them. I worked with HR and convinced them performance reviews were a useless relic of the past. I don't want to evaluate or label people. What do you want to get out of performance reviews?"

"Me, I don't want anything out of them. I do performance reviews for HR." Bill was as sure of this as he was of the fact that he needed liquid courage to write them.

"That's nonsense. You have one-on-ones, right?"

"Well, I mostly have them. I mostly have them every other week." He paused. "Well, sometimes every three weeks."

Jan gave him the what-are-you-thinking look. "That's a problem. If you don't have regular one-on-ones, you can't do performance reviews. But the problem isn't the review. The problem is feedback and building a trusting relationship, isn't it?"

Bill nodded. "I think I have that. Well, maybe not with the people I only see once every three weeks." He sighed.

"The idea behind a performance review is that you offer feedback to your employee," Jan said. "Well, and some people think it's useful to evaluate people and judge them against each other." She rolled her eyes. "Now that we use agile approaches, do you have any idea what your people are doing daily? Do you have the data to evaluate them?"

Bill shook his head. "Uh, no. They work independently from me as part of a team. Sure, if they need me, I help. But I don't help much anymore." He paused. "I don't think I can evaluate them. That's why I came to see you, to see what you're doing."

Jan shook her head. "Okay, so why would you do performance reviews?"

"I guess I can't," Bill said.

"Exactly. You need the team to offer feedback to each other. Do they know how to do that?"

"Sure. The team has been practicing their feedback all along. When one of them isn't sure how to say something, I've coached them. Sometimes I even suggest the right words to use."

"Excellent. So do you need to write a performance review for anyone your team?" Jan asked.

Bill thought for a minute. "No. Everyone here works together on one cross-functional team. But I have a few people in Colorado who work as a group and are not part of a cross-functional team. What do I do about them?"

"Whom do those people work with? Can those people ask for feedback from the people they work with?"

"Sure, I guess they can."

"The question is this: What value do you add as a manager in this equation? Can you possibly know enough about what these people do to provide them feedback? Is evaluating them useful at all? Or are you just mucking up the works?"

"Hmm, I think I'm mucking up the works," Bill admitted. "But what do I do instead?"

"How about you provide them feedback about the work you can see? Maybe even the work you can see that they perform as a team? Don't people want to know where they stand?" Jan asked.

"Well, they want to know where they stand relative to one another, right?"

Jan took a deep breath. "No. Do you want to know where you stand in relation to all the other managers?"

Bill thought for a second and said, "No, I guess not. I was going to say I thought I was a great manager. But from the questions you're asking me, I guess I'm not. I don't really want to know where I rank in the manager list."

"Exactly," Jan said. "People need feedback. They don't need ranking. Besides, how can you rank testers against developers against business analysts or product owners? They all work as an interdependent team. You can't say, 'This person is number one. This person is number two.' That's craziness."

Bill slowly nodded his head. "Okay, I see where you're headed."

"People do need feedback from the people they work with. Do you work with them?" Jan persisted.

"No."

"Okay. Then how do you propose to give them feedback, especially when you haven't been keeping up with the one-on-ones?"

"Okay, Jan, you've convinced me. Now, how do I convince HR?"

"I know just how to do this. Come with me."

If you want the short answer for stopping performance reviews, here's the brief answer.

As a manager, you create an environment of autonomy, mastery, and purpose. Maintain a cadence of one-on-ones, and create a job ladder or career paths that offer people opportunities to learn more.

When managers focus on creating opportunities for people and teams, they don't have to do performance reviews. The environment creates its own positive feedback loop. There's more about this topic in Book 3.

8.2 Avoid Evaluation or Grading People

Everyone needs feedback about their work. If you've done something great, you need to know—sooner rather than later. And if you've done something that wasn't great, you need to know that, too.

People don't need evaluation, such as "meets expectations." They don't need a grade, such as "3 out of 5."

I don't know about you, but the one time I received a "meets expectations," I was furious. I'd worked hard. Why did I only "meet expectations"? Because my boss had higher expectations of me than my peers. It didn't matter that we were at the same level on the career ladder. He expected more of *me.*

I soon left that organization. My boss didn't meet my expectations.

Each person in your organization offers something unique to the organization. People are not cogs. They are not interchangeable. That means you can't compare them to each other, one of the horrible things performance reviews tend to do.

You've probably heard of organizations where they expect everyone to be on a curve—10% of the people below average, 80% average, and 10% above average. How does that possibly account for or create an organization where people collaborate and learn?

When we evaluate and rank people against each other, we make psychological safety difficult, if not impossible. When we evaluate, we reinforce resource efficiency thinking. Evaluation reinforces Theory X management, which means managers control other people, not serve them.

Don't expect a successful collaborative or agile approach in your organization if you evaluate people by *their* contributions.

8.3 Self-Assessment Doesn't Work, Either

We, as humans, are not so good at assessing ourselves, either. We are subject to the Dunning-Kruger effect, a cognitive bias where incompetent people overestimate their skills. They believe they are actually competent or even superior. To make matters worse, they do not recognize these skills in other people. (There's some fascinating research in *I'd like to thank . . . myself.*[1] The smaller

---

[1] https://www.sciencedaily.com/releases/2016/03/160307152832.htm

the team—fewer than eight people—the more accurate our self-assessment can be.)

On the other hand, some competent people suffer from Imposter Syndrome, where they feel as if they are not competent and not responsible for their success. (I sometimes suspect that only the competent people ever suffer from Imposter Syndrome.)

If you can't judge people or look for self-assessment, how do you help people see when they're succeeding and when they're not?

You pay attention to what you can see.

8.4 Attention Works

Managers might not have a lot of time to see what people do. When you can pay attention, you might create the Hawthorne Effect. People do change their behavior when they know you're looking.

You can use the Hawthorne Effect to your advantage and offer reinforcing feedback. When you do, people can build on what they do well. That's paying attention to people, in the best possible sense.

In *Nine Lies About Work* [BUG19], Buckingham and Goodall say this:

> *Positive attention . . . is thirty times more powerful than negative attention in creating high performance on a team.*

Negative attention is change-focused feedback.

What if you serve an agile team? You help the people on the team learn to offer feedback and coaching to each other. You might practice feedback and coaching with them, so they learn how to offer feedback and coaching. (See *Create Your Successful Agile Project: Collaborate, Measure, Estimate, Deliver* [ROT17] for details about how you might start.)

As a leader, your role is to create an environment so people can change small problems before those problems become significant.

If you can help people see and change their behavior in two days, you don't have a two-week problem or a two-month problem. It's certainly not something that has remained on someone's "file" for the past year.

8.5 Feedback is a Culture Problem

How safe do you feel to offer any kind of feedback to your peers? How about to your managers? And, to the people you serve?

If you feel safe to offer feedback all around the organization, your managers designed the organization to enhance feedback.

If you don't feel safe to offer feedback? That's an organizational culture problem.

Managers can create a culture of feedback if they teach how to offer feedback—and model how to accept feedback. Managers can coach people on how to use which words and when. They can provide an environment in which it's safe to give and receive feedback. They can work with HR to eliminate the ranking system inherent in performance reviews.

Evaluation, with the inevitable ranking, destroys a team's ability to work together. Feedback can enhance it. Which would you choose?

8.5.1 *Consider This Design for a Feedback Lab*

I use feedback labs to teach people how to offer and receive feedback. Here's the agenda:

1. Each person spends a few minutes writing down at least three feedback scenarios they want to practice.
2. Ask the people to organize themselves into triads: person who offers the feedback, person who receives feedback, and an observer.
3. Now, spend seven minutes role-playing. I set the stage by saying, "Act the way you would act if you received this feedback. Don't make this more difficult than it has to be."
4. At the end of the seven minutes, ask the observer to offer feedback to the two other people. And, the person who received the feedback can offer their feedback after the observer.

5. Rotate places. Do another seven minutes followed by three minutes of feedback.
6. Rotate places again for the feedback and observations.

At the end of these rotations, each person had a chance to participate in each of the roles. Ask people what they noticed about the feedback, what felt easy and challenging, what they learned, and what they might do in the future.

You can use this design for a coaching lab, also.

The more people practice feedback, the easier it is to offer reinforcing feedback. And, when necessary, change-focused feedback.

The more the team can offer feedback to its members, the less you will have to do to "manage performance."

8.6 Options Instead of Performance Reviews

Performance reviews don't work.

We have decades of data that performance reviews don't work. They don't work for feedback. They don't work to "manage performance." They don't work to rank people. They don't work to manage salary expenses. They don't create parity.

Remember this: Environment Shapes Behavior on page 11. And, the manager's job is to create an environment where everyone can do their best work.

Don't use the yearly performance review to assess or evaluate a person's performance. You can't see the totality of a person's contribution to the greater effort.

What if you can't eliminate performance reviews? Consider these options while you—or preferably several people at the highest levels of management—nurture the organization's change to eliminate performance reviews:

- Build an effective relationship with everyone you serve. That way, if you see something not quite right, you can offer feedback and help the person get back on track. Even better, if you see something the person does well, you can offer reinforcing feedback as often as possible.

- Teach the people you serve how to offer feedback. Consider training or an all-team practice day (or days), so everyone learns and practices effective feedback and coaching.
- Focus on appreciations and reinforcing feedback over any other feedback.

If you feel you must live with your performance system, use some sort of outcome-based appraisal and *jointly* discuss a person's performance at every one-on-one. Make sure no one ever feels surprised by any performance evaluation. You might learn more about the environment than the person learns about his or her performance.

In addition,

- Work with HR to make sure your organization has a reasonable career ladder, so people know what they need to do to get to where they want to be.
- Work with HR to assess your salary levels inside the company and outside the company to make sure your entire organization is competitive.

In the past, I asked the people I served to offer me feedback on my management performance. At the time, I allowed them to offer anonymous feedback. I no longer believe anonymous feedback is best. I prefer transparent feedback.

When people know *everyone* can see their feedback, they tend to be more honest. I can't guarantee your results. You might consider an experiment to see your outcomes.

If your organization has a culture of performance reviews, you might need to address that first. The more you are supposed to evaluate a person based on his or her individual contributions, the less you Encourage Flow Efficiency on page 2 and trust across the organization.

The more your organization believes in performance reviews, the more Theory X (fear-based) the culture is, and the less Theory Y (respect-based).

Deming's 12th point (see *The Essential Deming: Leadership Principles from the Father of Quality* DEM13 is:

. . . Eliminate the annual rating or merit system.

Performance reviews don't work because Environment Shapes Behavior on page 11. Deming was correct. See what you can do to eliminate performance reviews.

When I speak about this, people want references right away. If you are one of these people, read these references. They are all in the bibliography, also.

- *First, Break All the Rules: What the World's Greatest Managers Do Differently* [BUC99].
- *Nine Lies About Work* [BUG19].
- Hope, Jeremy and Robin Fraser, *Beyond Budgeting: How Managers Can Break Free from the Annual Performance Trap* (Harvard Business Press, 2003).
- Kohn, Alfie, *Punished by Rewards* (New York: Houghton-Mifflin, 1993).
- Pfeffer, Jeffrey, *The Human Equation: Building Profits by Putting People First* (Boston: Harvard Business School Press, 1998).
- Pfeffer, Jeffrey, *What Were They Thinking? Unconventional Wisdom About Management* (Boston: Harvard Business School Press, 2007).
- Pfeffer, Jeffrey and Robert I. Sutton, *Hard Facts, Dangerous Half-Truths And Total Nonsense: Profiting From Evidence-based Management* (Boston: Harvard Business School Press, 2006).
- Hope, Jeremy, and Steve Player. *Beyond Performance Management: Why, When and How to Use 40 Tools and Best*

Practices for Superior Business Performance. Harvard Business Review Press, Boston, MA. 2012.

- Chandler, Tamra M. *How Performance Management is Killing Performance—and What to Do About It.* Berrett-Koehler Publishers, Inc. 2016.
- Austin, Robert D. *Measuring and Managing Performance in Organizations.* Dorset House Publishing, New York. 1996.

CHAPTER 9

Do People Ever Need External Credit?

While people don't usually benefit from performance reviews, your bosses need to know how the people you serve excel.

I had a boss who was great at saying, "Terri did this. Jen did that. JR did this other thing." We were each on different projects. We got to learn where we had succeeded. We felt great.

Not only did *we* know where we had succeeded, but my boss also told *her* bosses. When she told her bosses, I had opportunities to grow and try other roles in the organization. I had earned those opportunities. But, if my boss hadn't told her management team, they might not have *known* I had the abilities the roles needed.

As members of a group, we trusted each other. We were loyal to that boss. And, we were loyal to the company because we felt the appreciation.

Contrast that with some other places I've worked or consulted, especially where Theory X (fear-based) management still had a foothold.

Years ago, I worked with several people across the Engineering organization, trying to define their "best" project approach. They soon realized they needed several approaches, loosely based on size and complexity. You might recognize these as various agile and lean approaches now.

As a consultant, I reported to Mary, the Director of Process and Quality. I had one-on-ones with Mary every other week or so during the engagement. I explained who'd had great ideas every time we met.

She asked me once, "Does anyone *not* have great ideas?"

I sat back. After thinking, I said, "No, I don't think so." I ticked off the people on the committee and reminded her of their various ideas.

"If they're so good, what are you doing?"

Uh-oh. Mary might not see the value of the work I did. I explained that I facilitated their thinking, helping them generate ideas. Once we had those possibilities, I facilitated their assessment of those options. When would each option work or not work? And, I helped them create action items so they could test their ideas.

I explained all that to her. I said, "I'm sort-of your proxy. Just as you wouldn't tell them what to do, I don't either. We want them to generate and then commit to these various approaches, right?"

Mary nodded. "Yes, we do."

"So, if it's *my* work, why would they use it?"

She shook her head. "They wouldn't."

"Right. So, since it's the team's work, they need to get the credit for it. I get credit for coaching the team. And, some individual coaching. But they get the credit for everything else."

Mary smiled. "You also get credit for this coaching, too. I'm not sure I would have thought of that without you telling me."

Mary changed how she served the people who worked with her that day. She'd thought she needed to take credit for their work. Once Mary realized she would look even better if she told everyone else about this team, she felt freer.

Mary didn't have to focus on *their* work. She could give credit, and her bosses would realize how smart she was for hiring these people.

When you give credit to the people you serve, their work reflects on you.

9.1 Myth: People Don't Need Credit

"Robert, do you have a minute?" Cheryl, the development manager, stood at her director's door.

"Sure, let me save this." Robert stopped what he was doing. "You look worried. Come on over, and let's sit at the visitor's table. You look serious."

"Well, it is. I'm not sure how to say it, so I'll just spit it out."

Robert nodded.

Cheryl took a deep breath. "You remember the big push to finish the release last month? We've almost got our agile approach, but our transformation is pretty shaky. We actually pulled some overtime, which we're not supposed to do. We didn't extend our timebox, but not everyone worked just forty hours a week. Some people worked close to sixty hours the entire timebox. It was a very tough two-week iteration."

"Yup," Robert said. "I've been trying to smooth our agile transformation, but it's really hard work."

Cheryl nodded. "You came around to our demo, which was great. The team appreciated your thanks. You even wrote individual thank-you email notes. It looked like you understood what the team did."

She paused and then continued. "But you took credit for what the team did at the Ops meeting. At least, that's what it seemed like to me and everyone on the team. Maybe you can tell me what happened. I'm upset, and I didn't even realize it had happened. Someone on the team read the public minutes, so now the team is upset. Please tell me what happened."

Robert shook his head. "Oh, boy, that's not what I intended at all. But I can understand that's how it came across." He swallowed and continued. "At the Ops meeting, all the directors explain how their projects and programs are proceeding. You know that, right?"

Cheryl nodded.

"Well, they were in a rush to finish at the Ops meeting. What a surprise. So they wanted to timebox everyone's reports. I had five minutes to report on your team's work and everyone else's work. I did. And I'm not in charge of the minutes. I probably said something like, "We finished the release on time." I didn't say,

"The team completed the release on time" to clarify that the team had done it. I wasn't clear because I was rushing. And the minutes reflected that."

Cheryl sat back in her chair.

"I was not trying to take away credit from your team," Robert said. "I was not trying to take the credit myself. I can see how it looked. I hadn't even looked at the Ops minutes." He paused. "Now that our agile culture makes everything more transparent, I'd better take a look at these things. I can see why you're upset and why the team is upset. Let me fix the minutes and apologize to the team."

Cheryl smiled, just a bit.

"I do not want to take credit for things I had nothing to do with," Robert said.

"Thanks," Cheryl said. "I realize this might sound like a small thing, but it's not a small thing to the team. These folks worked really hard. You didn't work on their project. They were quite surprised to see you associated with the project."

Robert smiled and said, "Well, you are in my organization. But, no, I had nothing to do with your project."

Cheryl grinned and sat back in her chair.

Robert continued. "I'll fix the minutes. How about if I stop by the team room today? Will that help?"

"An email would be great, too," Cheryl suggested.

"OK, I'll do both."

9.2 Always Give Credit for Work Other People Perform

As a manager, make sure you know who performed the work and make sure other people know, too. It seems like a small thing, but it's huge for the people who did the work.

People want to know you appreciate them. They want to know you are willing to carry that appreciation up the corporate hierarchy.

More importantly, they want to know you are not a jerk who will take credit for the work they perform.

Miscommunications can occur, and when they do, you should straighten them out right away if you know about them.

9.3 Fix Miscommunications When They Occur

We're people, so we create miscommunications. People say the wrong things. People take minutes incorrectly. People hear the wrong things. Whatever the problem is, communications slip-ups will happen. And you will need to recover.

When a communications problem happens, make sure you explain your appreciation to the people who did that great job, and to the people who should have known that the people did that great job. Choose your words with care. This time, write your words down and send an email, write a memo, or fix the minutes of a meeting. You want a record of this so that people will be able to find the electronic or written archive of the conversation they hear.

9.4 Consider Formal Appreciations

An appreciation is a personalized thank-you. It works quite well for individuals. Don't use it for teams. It loses its power when you try to use it for multiple people at once.

Here is an appreciation:

"First name," I appreciate you for the "specific thing the person did." It gave me "some specific benefit to me."

You can see that an appreciation, offered in private, one at a time to specific people, is a powerful way to reinforce the behavior you find valuable.

Here, Robert could say to Cheryl, "Cheryl, I appreciate you for the courage it took to say this to me. It allowed me to fix this before it became a huge problem and blew up in my face. Thank you for having my back."

9.5 Taking Credit is Anti-Delegation

You might work for someone who wants to extend you all the credit for the work, not the team. You might even be tempted to take it.

Beware of taking credit, even on behalf of your team.

When you take credit instead of offering the credit, you lose your integrity. Without integrity, people lose trust in you.

When people discover you took credit, they might not be so responsive the next time you attempt to extend them autonomy or when you try to delegate work to them. As one developer said to me at a client site, "Why should I make my manager look good when he doesn't make me look good?"

9.6 When You Give Credit, You Look Like a Star

When you give credit to other people, you look like a star to the rest of the organization. Even if you didn't hire the people who are doing a stellar job, you're managing them in some way that allows them to be great. The more the people who work for you are doing great work, the better you look.

And the more you look like you don't have to work hard to manage them, the better you are as a manager—and the better you look.

Give credit generously. It doesn't cost anything and buys you a tremendous amount of respect and goodwill.

9.7 Options to Start Offering Credit

Consider these ideas to start acknowledging people's work:

1. Offer reinforcing feedback to individuals, when you see them doing something right. Consider offering this feedback privately.
2. Offer reinforcing feedback to teams, when you see them doing something right.
3. Offer credit to *teams* in public. The more you offer public credit to teams, the more you reinforce an environment of teamwork.

CHAPTER 10

Who Deserves a Job Here?

Have you been in a position where you—or your manager—wanted to save a problematic employee? Maybe you felt as if you bent over backward to keep an employee? Even if you knew that person wasn't helping, you might have felt guilty about "pushing" a person out.

I've met managers who feel guilty that they aren't able to help the person perform the necessary work. Some managers think they can spend more and more time with the person who can't do the job. Other managers believe they owe the person feedback and coaching for a year. And if the person still can't perform the job? Too many managers I coach feel guilty they couldn't turn this person's performance around.

Your job as a manager is to create a harmonic whole. That means you do what you can to help the people you serve. All the people you serve need to fulfill both the technical and interpersonal parts of their jobs. If anyone can't, your job is to help that person move out of the organization.

Don't placate a person who can't do the job.

The faster you act to either help a person succeed or move the person out, the better a manager you are. You're serving the harmonic whole.

Not every employee has a place at every organization. If you help someone find a new job elsewhere in your organization or outside your organization, everyone will be happier. You'll free a bunch of your management time. The team will be thrilled they don't have to work around a problematic person.

And, every time I've helped someone find a new role somewhere else, that person has thanked me. You might experience the same.

10.1 Myth: I Can Save Everyone

"Everyone is worth saving. Everyone is worth saving." Jimmy muttered under his breath as he walked into my office. "Hi, Steve. I'm here for our one-on-one. I have a real problem."

"OK, let's hear it."

"Frieda is a problem in my group."

"Jimmy, we have discussed Frieda before. I thought you were going to put her on a get-well plan last week."

"But, Steve, everyone is worth saving!"

"Jimmy, listen to me. It's time to do a little addition. How many people do you have in your group?"

"Eight."

"And how much time do you have to spend with them in a week?"

"About twelve hours total. That's it."

"How much time have you spent with each of them this past week?"

"Um, I have to think." Jimmy spent a few seconds thinking. Then he stopped and paled. "I haven't spent time with anyone except Frieda."

"So, you have spent all of your time with the person who is delivering the least, right?"

Jimmy nodded.

"And none of your time with the people who deliver the most, right?"

Jimmy nodded again.

"Does that sound reasonable to you?"

Jimmy slowly shook his head.

"So why do you think you can save everyone? Why do you think everyone is worth saving?"

Jimmy sighed. "Steve, Frieda is a smart person. She's nice."

Steve agreed and nodded. "She is smart. Nice? In some circumstances."

"She needs a job," Jimmy said.

Steve cocked his head to the side. "Jimmy, we are not running a charity. Frieda does need a job, but she doesn't need a job from us."

"Steve, I don't know what to do."

"Jimmy, you *do* know what to do; we've discussed it. You don't want to help Frieda leave because you think you will be a bad guy, and it goes against your values. I've offered to help you, and you've turned me down. Twice. Now, you either let me help you today, or I'll do it myself. You came in here muttering 'Everyone is worth saving' as if you were going to convince me. You are not going to convince me."

Jimmy sighed.

Steve continued. "But I've called Tranh over at our competitor. He is interested in Frieda's resume. He knows that we've had trouble with her, and he's still interested. Now, are you going to start the get-well plan, or am I?"

10.2 Why Can't You Save Everyone?

Employees don't succeed for any number of reasons.

Often, it's a cultural fit problem you didn't catch during the interview. But even if it's not cultural fit, if you've provided honest and open feedback and the employee can't or won't change, it's up to the manager, or the self-managing team, to help the employee move on.

When Your Company Can't or Won't Act

Some organizations fear firing a person. Or, they say, "We never fire or lay anyone off." If you have that problem, you might not be able to help a person leave your team. Your company won't act to support you.

You have choices. Never give the person a raise or a promotion—not even a cost-of-living raise. Remove that person from your team. Even if you have nothing for that person to do, do not let that person join a team.

When companies feel as if they "can't do anything," they actively create a placating culture. They are willing to pay the person's salary so they don't have to act. You can act in the small, for your team or department, instead of for the greater whole. However, your job is to create a harmonic whole. If one of the people you serve cannot create that whole, prevent them from creating disharmony.

Every time I've had to fire someone, I retrospected on the issues. How could I have handled it differently, from hiring to firing? I often think of having to fire someone as a management mistake. Yes, managers make mistakes and we need to acknowledge them and move on. That's one of the reasons I like to help an employee move on.

You might help an employee move to another group that's a better fit if you have a sufficiently large organization. But you might have to help someone leave the company altogether.

10.3 Why Help an Employee Leave Your Team?

When someone isn't working out, that person might "unjell" the entire team, the person might prevent the project from making progress technically, or the person might not do any work. I've seen all three of these problems.

In this case, when Frieda didn't get her way, she was an unjeller. When she attempted to participate in a meeting, she managed to push people farther apart.

Frieda's actions decreased the team's psychological safety.

For example, one problem Frieda's team was trying to solve was scheduling lab time. With Frieda, the team was unable to brainstorm solutions and come to a decision. First, team members were unable to stick to their timebox for generating ideas, because, during the brainstorming, Frieda wanted to discuss the solutions, even when the designated facilitator explained they were generating possibilities.

The team eliminated several possibilities. Then, the team moved to elaborate on the remaining ideas. However, Frieda kept returning to some of the discarded ideas. "But those were good ideas," she protested. The facilitator decided to discuss Frieda's meeting behavior with her. "Frieda, if you can't stick with our process, I want you to leave the meeting."

"But, I have to use the lab, too."

"But we all agreed we finished generating ideas. It's time for us to discuss *these* ideas."

"But I like *that* idea. I don't care if I agreed before. I like that idea now."

One of the other meeting participants said, "I'm leaving. This meeting is a waste of my time." Two of the other three people left also.

Frieda had exhibited meeting behavior like this before. Her colleagues were no longer willing to work with her again for problem-solving.

When a team has a problem-solving meeting, and team members can't solve a problem because of one person, they have to solve the team membership problem first.

10.4 Understand Team "Fairness"

Jimmy, the manager, was concerned about being "fair" and "nice" to Frieda. He'd temporarily forgotten the rest of the team. He felt as if he wasn't fair to Frieda, but the real problem was that Jimmy was beyond fair to Frieda—and he wasn't fair to the rest of the team.

He was incongruent, placating Frieda. He didn't create an environment where the entire team could thrive.

When you manage team membership, you might not feel as if you are fair to the person you are helping to leave, but you are. And, you are fair to the rest of the team.

Your team's members might be feeling many things: They may feel betrayed for the lack of your attention or for the amount of attention you are spending on the employee who is not working out. Those team members might be wondering if you can even see the problems. Or they might think you don't care about them.

You don't know what the team members think unless you ask them. In my experience, the other team members feel frustration with the slow-to-act manager.

The faster you manage the issues around an unjeller, or any other team membership problem, the faster the team will thank you. You can help the team by assisting the team members learn to offer feedback and coaching themselves. And, by practicing with you, if they like.

I prefer it when the team can solve its membership problems. That doesn't always work. When it doesn't, the manager must solve team problems.

If the team can't work as a team, you're not doing your job as a manager.

When you help an employee move out of a team—especially one who is an unjeller like Frieda—you help the team. Team members will become more energized, happier, and freer. And their outcomes will increase. Why? Because the unjeller no longer prevents the entire team from collaborating. The team can create or restore psychological safety.

10.5 Consider When You Should Save an Employee

Think twice or even three times before you spend a lot of time to "save" a problematic employee.

Not every employee has a place in your organization:

- Does this person fit the culture?
- Does the organization still need someone in this role?
- Does the person have to change how he or she works to better work with the team?

If it's a question of training, I much prefer to offer training to someone who fits the culture.

Here's the question I ask:

Am I better off with or without this person?

Here's how I frame my thinking about the "better off" question:

1. Does this person fit the culture? Can they work within the organization's and team's stated working agreements? If they can, I continue. If not, I work to help them leave. For example, I once helped a quite-directive manager find a job elsewhere so I could replace him with a more collaborative manager.
2. Does this person have sufficient interpersonal skills? Many people in high tech don't have excellent interpersonal skills. However, if they have the minimum, maybe I can find a role where they can succeed. If the person is willing to work on their behaviors, I'll try that, too. If the person doesn't have the minimum interpersonal skills, I help them leave. One developer had only two modes: he either yelled at or blamed other people when things didn't work. I helped him find a new position outside the company.
3. Can they do the technical work? If they only need some training, I work to get them training and coaching. However, if I haven't seen any evidence of their technical abilities, and I've offered training and coaching, then I help them find a new role elsewhere. I've had a lot of good results assisting people to learn new technical skills for development, testing, and management.
4. Is the person interested in changing their skills: interpersonal or technical? If not, I help them find a new job. If I decide that

this person might add value, I create an action plan, so we both know how to define success and see change. I've only had one developer and one tester not want to learn new skills.

Are you worried about helping a person find a new role elsewhere? When I realized how valuable I could be to the people who didn't fit, I changed my mind.

10.6 Create Action Plans

If you decide to save someone, you (or someone you ask) commit to investing a lot of time in that person's growth. I prefer to limit the amount of time I spend on investing in someone else's growth.

I tend to timebox action plans to between six and eight weeks. Depending on the work, you might need to offer more or less time. For example, if you arrange for training, you might not be able to start the action plan until the person has completed training.

Consider creating an action plan with:

- Weekly deliverables that are either done or not done. The deliverables need clear criteria, so everyone can see and agree on the person's progress. Or, lack thereof.
- Consider "plan to leave" decision points in the action plan. How will you handle any of these possibilities:
  – If the person no longer wants to continue with the action plan?
  – If the person cannot deliver any of the deliverables?
- Define your agreement for helping the person find another role.

One last note about these action plans: anytime I've had trouble gaining agreement on the weekly deliverables, I've soon realized the person either couldn't fit with the culture or didn't have enough technical skills to succeed.

I've succeeded several times helping those people find other jobs.

10.7 Help the Person Succeed Elsewhere

One of the first times I spoke publicly about this, one of the audience members had a question: "Where do you help the other person look for a job?"

My answer, which surprised everyone, was, "At a competitor."

The room erupted in laughter, which surprised me. I was serious. Why? Because the person might have industry skills that might be transferable to the competitor.

Long ago, I worked in a variety of machine vision companies in the Boston area. We all knew about each other. Many of us managers knew each other. The industry wasn't that big at the time.

One of my testers didn't fit the culture. I called my counterpart manager—so he could hear the sincerity in my voice—and told him I had a person who didn't fit. Was he interested in the tester?

We spoke for a few minutes, and yes, the other manager was interested. The competitor interviewed the tester, made an offer, and the tester left inside of two weeks.

That approach might not fit for you. But, do consider helping the person find a new role, sooner rather than later. That might mean you offer to write a reference—and clarify what you will and won't say. You might offer the names of recruiters, or introductions to other managers elsewhere.

Decide what fits for you.

However, do not keep people around because you feel sorry for them. The good people will leave. The people who remain can't deliver and can't interact with the people around them.

10.8 Act Promptly

If you need to help someone leave, don't let the situation fester. The longer it takes you to act, the less respect the remaining people have for you. You can't discuss your actions with the rest of the people, but you can act promptly.

You can help an employee exit gracefully. If you are part of a large organization, and there is another place for your employee, help your employee transfer. But don't make your headache someone else's problem. I've interviewed people who had twenty years of the same year of experience because their managers handed them off to a different department, because the company was large enough. No manager ever took the courageous effort of helping the employee out the door.

If you are lucky and you have checked with your colleagues at your competitors, you might be able to find a place for your employee at another organization. Even if you cannot help your employee leave.

Not every employee is salvageable at *your* organization. It's almost always a case of cultural fit. You can prevent these problems by discovering them during hiring. If you discover problems after you hire someone, don't let the problems fester.

As soon as you realize you have a problem, offer the employee feedback. If that doesn't work, help your problem employee out the door. Your headaches will go away, and your team will thank you.

10.9 Options to Decide Who Deserves a Job Here

Consider these ideas for who you want to continue to work with:

1. Make sure you've offered specific feedback. See Do I Really Need to Tell Someone How They're Doing? on page 41.
2. If you have offered feedback and coaching, and maybe some training, move to the next question. Ask the person, "Do you want to continue to work here?" Sometimes, the person will say no. You can then ask, "How can I support you in finding another job?"
3. Many organizations have rules and policies about how to help people find another job elsewhere. Remove that person from the rest of the team. And, help the people who create the policies realize they are asking you to pay a yearly salary for someone to do nothing. (See the issues in Why Can't You Save Everyone? on page 111.)

CHAPTER 11

Do Hiring Shortcuts Work?

Too many managers leave too much of the hiring process to HR. That means they don't know how to define a job or interview well. And, too many HR people don't understand how knowledge workers work—the HR people fall into too many hiring traps.

Watch for your hiring shortcuts. Remember that hiring a person is the most important job a manager can do. That person will either reinforce your culture and help create a harmonic whole—or make life miserable for other people.

When I hire, I hire people to reinforce the culture I want—not necessarily the current culture. For example, do I want people who will challenge a current team with new ideas? That might be both what people can discuss and how people treat each other. Do I want more perspectives on the customers, the products, and how we work? That's part of what people can discuss and how people can treat each other. As a manager, what behaviors do I want to reinforce now and in the future? (See Managers Create and Refine the Culture on page 14 for more details.)

11.1 Myth: We Can Take Hiring Shortcuts

"Hey, Stan." Tricia entered her CIO, Stan's, office and sat down in his visitor chair.

"Hi, Tricia, I'm so glad you're early for our one-on-one today," Stan said. "We need to talk about hiring. I finally have approval for those testers you've been after me to hire." Stan walked around his visitor table and closed the door.

Tricia smiled, internally giving herself a high five. "Okay, I'll start the job analysis and then work with each of the teams. I'm ready for our next item."

"Wait a minute. You don't need to take that long, do you? It sounds like a lot of work and aggravation for not much return. You just have to hire people who can type, right?"

Tricia looked at Stan and started counting to ten in her head. "Stan, you know we're agile, right? You know that our testers do more than type, right? They always have."

"Tricia, you are so easy!" Stan grinned.

Tricia made a face at him. "Okay, but the teams aren't falling for any of the hiring traps: barrel-of-the-bottom candidates, supposed 'rock stars' or 'ninjas,' not paying people what they're worth, or people who don't fit with the team. And we can't ignore the time it takes us to hire people. You didn't get the approval in time. The teams have been limping along without the people they need. It's almost a crisis now. I was going to ask you for approval to hire contractors. But they would need to fit with the team, anyway."

"I didn't realize there were so many hiring traps," Stan mused. "I was only joking."

"Hardy har har. That's me laughing at you," Tricia said. "There are a ton of traps. We need people to work together and feel good about their team. This hiring work is hard."

Stan nodded.

"Interviewing will take time away from feature development," Tricia continued. "I'll be spending time phone-screening candidates. I don't mind doing it, because it will save the team's time. I might work with the other managers or leads to help them learn. I'm not sure how this will work."

Stan said, "Please do. You have a more rigorous approach to hiring than any of the other managers here."

"Thanks," Tricia said. "I do that because we both know that hiring a person is the most costly and the biggest point of leverage we have

in our organization. We want to make each hire great. I'll start now."
She paused. "Okay, what's next on our list?"

11.2 See Typical Hiring Shortcuts

If you are a senior manager and you approve a req, it's tempting to
"help" another manager by giving that manager a hiring shortcut.
But a shortcut is almost always a hiring trap—and there are plenty of
hiring pitfalls. Here are a few shortcuts you might have seen.

11.2.1 *Below Average People*

One common hiring trap is to think that you can hire from the "bottom
of the barrel" to save money on salaries. I once consulted for a company
that wanted to decrease the cost of their development. They purposely
hired developers who were below average. They paid below-average
salaries. And the product? Way below average.

By the time they'd been in business for about ten years, their code
and tests were a disaster. What should have taken them days or weeks
took months to do.

The people didn't have the technical ability to work themselves
out of the debt they had built because they had consistently created
a culture of below-average people hiring people who were even less
capable than the hiring managers and teams.

11.2.2 *"Rock Stars"*

You might think I'm suggesting you only hire "rock stars" or "ninjas"
or "gurus." No, I'm not suggesting that, either. I am not a fan of people
who call themselves any one of those titles.

When a person calls him- or herself a rock star, ninja, or guru, I
wonder about that person's capability to learn or become a part of a
team. I once worked with a person who called himself the "code czar."
Yes, that was the title he gave himself. He decided it was his job to
"clean up" the code everyone else had checked in.

He destroyed the teamwork on that project, never mind any semblance of code understanding on the part of the authors. Would you like to work with someone like that?

Sometimes, you need people with great expertise. I am suggesting you find and hire people like that, but not people with so much hubris that they cannot work with mere mortals like the rest of us.

11.2.3 *Shopping List of Technical Skills*

Many organizations use Applicant Tracking Systems (ATS)—often, to stay within the law. However, many hiring managers and most HR professionals fall into the trap of creating a shopping list of technical skills. If a candidate can't check off all those boxes, no one looks at the candidate's resume.

Technical skills are the easiest skills to learn. You can teach someone the inside of an operating system, or the details of a new computer language.

Can you teach someone how to work as part of a team? Or, how to use their initiative to help the team discover new possibilities and experiment?

In my experience, interpersonal skills are at least as valuable as technical skills. And, they are much more difficult to teach. You can offer reinforcing feedback and coaching. And, if the person isn't interested in developing their interpersonal skills, you'll both be frustrated.

If you, as a leader, want to create a harmonic whole, a team who can focus on a purpose and work towards that purpose, you need people who can work together. A shopping list job description doesn't help you create that culture.

11.2.4 *Hire Too-Similar People*

I meet many managers who fall into the rut of hiring people who look like them, went to the same schools, and have similar experiences.

Each person might be quite smart. However, the team can't capitalize on those smarts to create great and innovative products.

Instead, when you include women (and other diversities), you are more likely to create a smart team. Anita Williams Woolley's article, *Evidence for a Collective Intelligence Factor in the Performance of Human Groups* [WOO10] explains that groups with more women performed better than less diverse groups.

I've found these approaches useful when I wanted to increase diversity in teams:

- Change your sourcing strategy. When I directed the recruiter to look elsewhere, I found a higher variety of people.
- Avoid shopping lists of technical skills.
- Become aware of your inherent biases. (We all have biases. The more aware we are about our biases, the easier we can manage them.)

In my experience, diverse teams create more fun in the workplace and work together well to create great products. (See *Hiring Geeks That Fit* [ROT12] for more details.)

11.2.5 *Wait for Perfection*

There are many traps when you wait for the perfect candidate. You might think, especially if some company in your town has had a massive layoff, "Oh, there are many great candidates to choose from. I can wait and find the perfect candidate."

There are probably many perfect candidates. Choose the first person who fits the team and proceed with your work.

The longer you wait to fill the position, the longer the team struggles with their current work. I once worked with a team that had been waiting for six months to find the "right" tester. The developers were developing system tests—not their expertise. They managed to miss some important problems, and they missed a crucial deadline in the market for the product. By the time they finally hired someone, they needed two more people to help them out of their testing debt.

The longer you wait for the perfect candidate, the more great candidates you miss. Don't hire someone inadequate; hire someone excellent. But that person doesn't have to be perfect.

Remember that none of us are perfect. Are you perfect? I'm not.

11.3 Offer a Candidate a Reasonable Salary

If you can bypass these hiring shortcuts, you probably have a reasonable candidate.

A job analysis will tell you what a job is worth to you. (See *Hiring Geeks That Fit* [ROT12] for details about job analysis.) Your HR department can help you see what the pay ranges might be for that job. Once you know that, you can offer a candidate a reasonable salary.

I've seen traps of offering either a too-low or a too-high salary based on a candidate's previous salary.

Here are the traps I've seen when you offer a too-low salary based on the candidate's previous salary:

- You may well encounter a pay parity problem within the department or company. If the person you offered a lower salary is part of a protected class, you leave the door open for a lawsuit.
- If you offer a lower salary because you think you can, you start the relationship without integrity and congruence.
- Your company might get a reputation as a place that lowballs candidates. If so, that reputation can take years to overcome.

And, the traps of offering a too-high salary because of a candidate's previous salary?

- You will encounter a pay parity problem within the department or the company. That's a timebomb for the next time you address salaries in the team, group, or department.

- When people realize this candidate makes more money, you'll create resentment inside the team. I have a story about this in Book 3. Yes, I left that company even though they gave me the "best" raise they could.
- It's incongruent. The organization creates an unsafe environment and creates distrust among the people who need to trust each other.

Know what the job is worth to you. Start with a job analysis so you know which skills are most important and then see what you are willing to offer as a pay range.

Start the relationship with integrity and congruence.

11.4 Hire for Cultural Fit

Culture is what your organization rewards, how people treat each other, and what you, at your organization, can discuss. It's not about who you would take on a desert island, or if you were an animal what that animal would be.

When you hire for cultural fit, you discover how a person works at work. You ask behavior-description questions. Behavior-description questions are open-ended questions where people tell you how they behaved in the past—the stories of their career. Behavior description questions are not hypothetical questions.

In addition, I like to create auditions that show you how a person will perform the work and interact with coworkers.

Many people think cultural fit is hiring for personality. It's not. Hiring for cultural fit is first assessing people's technical abilities to see if they have sufficient skills (not tools), then seeing if those people's interpersonal skills match the needs of the organization and the team. Note that if a person can't do the work, you don't have to bother looking at their cultural fit.

I wrote extensively about this particular problem in *Hiring Geeks That Fit* [ROT12].

11.5 Hiring Shortcuts Don't Help Anyone

Just because you got your job doesn't mean you know how to hire people. Learn everything you can and don't take a back seat to HR.

You can hire great people who fit the team and the organization. Once you find them, pay them according to the value they provide.

Then you can see the team make their magic.

Remember, hiring is the most significant leverage you have as a manager. Use that leverage wisely. When you and your team hire great people, you can reinforce respect, trust, and loyalty inside the team.

11.6 Options to Improve Your Hiring Practices

Consider these ideas to improve your hiring practices:

1. Review resumes as a team. For many years, as a hiring manager, I reviewed resumes with my fellow hiring managers. When I realized the team needed to learn how to review resumes, I started to review resumes with my team. I have found value in both practices.
2. Learn how to ask behavior-description questions and practice. When everyone learns to ask these questions, interviews become more valuable and more fun.
3. Learn how to create meaningful auditions. Not technical tests—auditions. I have yet to find value in a technical test, although many hiring managers tell me they have.
4. Make sure the team has the last word on hiring anyone for the team. Go against the team's recommendations at your peril.

As with all hiring approaches, your mileage will vary.

CHAPTER 12
Are People Resources?

The company I worked for was in financial trouble. My manager reviewed the org chart along with the budget. "I need to cut the budget. Which resources can we cut?"

"Well, I don't think we can cut software licenses." I was reviewing my copy of the budget. "I don't understand this overhead item here." I pointed to a particular line item.

"No," he said. "I'm talking about people. Which people can we lay off? We need to cut expenses."

I stopped and looked at him. "People aren't resources. People finish work. If you don't want us to finish projects, let's decide which projects not to do. Then we can reallocate people if we want. But we don't start with people. That's crazy."

My manager looked at me as if I'd grown three heads. "I'll start wherever I want," he said. He looked unhappy.

I asked, "What is the target you need to accomplish? Maybe we can ship something earlier, and bring in revenue, instead of laying people off? You know, bring up the top line, not decrease the bottom line?"

Now he looked at me as if I had four heads.

"Just tell me who to cut. We have too many resources."

When managers think of people as resources, they, too often, stop thinking. My manager was under pressure from his management to reduce his budget. In the same way that technical people under pressure to meet a date stop thinking, managers under pressure stop thinking.

Anyone under pressure stops thinking. We react. We can't consider options. That's because we are so very human.

People are resourceful. But we, the people, are not resources. We are not the same as desks, licenses, infrastructure, and other goods that people need to finish their work.

12.1 Myth: I Can Treat People as Interchangeable Resources

"David, I need a few things to make this program successful," Sherry, a program manager, explained to her VP. "I need a team room for the core team so we can keep our kanban board on the wall. I also want a dashboard wall. That way you can see what's going on."

David grinned. "I'm going to like this already. Okay, how about the Maui room?"

"You do realize I need this room for the entire duration of the program?"

"Yes. It's a resource you need, so it's yours."

"Excellent!" Sherry said. "Okay, let's go on to some people issues. Some of our feature teams are not quite fully staffed. We're short a tester here, a developer there. It's not a huge problem right now. It will be in a month. I need your support when I go talk to the managers. I'm in problem-understanding mode right now."

"Okay, I'll get you the resources you need."

Sherry paused for a moment. She said, "David, did you just call the people 'resources'?"

"Well, yes. Is that a problem?"

"To me, it is." Sherry paused, unsure if she should continue. *What the heck,* she thought. *Tell him what his language says about his assumptions.*

"When I think of resources, I think of desks, capital, software, hardware, infrastructure, and other things like that. *Things.* Not people. When you say 'resources,' your managers take their cues from you. For example, I mean full-time people, permanently assigned as full-time people on these teams. Is that what you mean?"

"Of course." David nodded in agreement.

"I bet that when you say 'resource,' not all your managers hear that," Sherry said. "I bet some of them hear FTE—full-time equivalent people. You and I both know that FTEs will not help this program."

David nodded. "You're right about that."

"We're going to have to show value from the start with this program," Sherry said. "It's going to be difficult. We need people who are committed to their teams. FTEs might be able to do that, but it would be so much more difficult. I want full-time people who are full-time committed to a specific team. Right?"

"Yup, I want full-time, committed teams, too," David said.

"Thinking about people as 'resources'—that's legacy language from command and control days. It's unfortunate that now we have 'Human Resources.' I liked it better when it was called 'Personnel,'" Sherry said.

They both smiled at that.

Sherry continued, "You might not even realize it. When you talk about 'resources' and you mean people, you dehumanize people. That doesn't create an excellent environment for our work. You can overcome that. But why should you have to? When you talk about FTEs, you—and worse, the finance people—assume a couple of things: that we can use part-time people; and that multiple people can effectively do the work of one person."

David raised one eyebrow.

"Now, when people pair or swarm, you do get multiple people working together," Sherry said. "That's collaboration. But that's not what this FTE business is all about. FTE work is when you have a part-time person on Monday and one on Tuesday and one on Wednesday and one on Thursday and one on Friday—and they may or may not coordinate their work. And supposedly they are all one FTE. You and

I both know that unless they coordinate their work, they are not one FTE. They need to coordinate and collaborate. It takes a lot of work for two people to be one FTE, never mind five people."

David shook his head. "Yeah, you're right."

"We don't have interchangeable people here," Sherry said. "We have unique people. We want teams that can work together. The people who do that are not resources. They are human beings."

"Okay," David said. "Got it. No more people as resources. Now, what else do you need for this program?"

12.2 People Accomplish Work

When managers—especially senior managers—look at an organization chart, they see names in boxes. If the organization is large enough, they don't even see names. That's a problem. They miss the fact that human beings are inside the boxes—or, more likely, working in the space between the boxes.

Think about the word *resource* and what it means. The dictionary defines a resource as the usefulness of something. Usefulness.

When managers use the word in organizations, they mean the ability of people to accomplish work. Accomplishment is not usefulness. Too often, accomplishment refers to outputs, not outcomes, what the organization needs.

It is useful for a person to accomplish work. But in software, we accomplish work in teams. Software is about learning through collaboration. Anything we do alone is interesting but not always pertinent to the work of the team.

I bet you have been in situations where you prototyped something alone, tried to bring it to the team's attention, and the team ignored you. However, if you prototype with a team—or even just one team member— the team is more likely to pay attention to your results. That is useful.

Alone, while we might be useful, we don't accomplish enough. Together, as a team, we finish work that aligns with the goals of the organization.

12.3 Language Matters

The language we use matters to everyone. I find it unfortunate that the department attending to employees is called "Human Resources." That language colors what managers call people in the organization. If HR calls people "resources," then it must be okay, right?

But the more you call people "resources," the more they *appear* to become interchangeable—and more like desks, or infrastructure, or something that is easily negotiable. One developer or tester looks just like another.

The fact that Tom is a wonderful facilitator and can ask great questions in a retrospective? When we use words such as "resource" to refer to people, Tom becomes interchangeable with Lakshmi, who is a focused, goal-oriented architect-type person who enjoys mentoring others.

Both are agile developers, and both are people you would want on your team, but they are very different developers and very different people who contribute differently.

People are resourceful. Because of their resourcefulness, we can create a more resilient organization that can achieve its goals.

12.4 People Are Also Not FTEs

FTE, Full-Time Equivalent, is another unfortunate term. When finance people talk about FTEs, they mean adding the hours of a person here and a person there and charging their work to your project. These people—who might work part-time—are not the same as one person, even if each of them is half-time.

You might only pay the salary equivalent of one person, but the fact is this: You and the people on the project communicate with two people.

Because people are not fungible (interchangeable), we can't think about people as FTEs. Each of us is a unique person with unique strengths and unique offerings for our work. Our uniqueness allows each of us to contribute differently.

Here's how I've described the problem of FTEs with Finance people and managers in the past:

- It's true that each person costs less than a full-time person. Let's call it half as much if people work half-time and we pay half benefits.
- If people work half-time, they spend half the time *away* from the team. They don't have the context of learning with the team.
- That means that each time these people return to the team, the team needs to reintegrate the part-time people.

Then, I can talk about the problems of multitasking, where people lose the context and make mistakes. In my experience, a person loses 10-40% of their time to reintegrating the new team's context.

But don't make the mistake that people are FTEs; they're not. People are people.

12.5 People Are Not Resources

Let's change the language in our organizations. Let's stop talking about people as "resources" and start talking about people as people. We might still need layoffs. But, maybe we can handle them with humanity. Perhaps we can think of the work strategically.

We disrespect people when we refer to them as resources. We're incongruent. We create a challenging environment for these human beings.

Think about what happens when we call people "resources":

- We remove their humanity, the characteristics that make people so valuable. Only people can learn. Only people can improve over time. Only people can apply their knowledge and their learning to create and support great products.
- We don't think about what people need for a great work environment. For example, people across a team all need access to the same tools. People need room to work alone, to work in pairs, and to work as teams.

- We're incongruent, thinking about ourselves and the context, not the other. That incongruence allows us to make challenging decisions, such as creating policies that make it difficult for people to work together. (See Book 3 for an extensive discussion of this challenge.)

When we disrespect people, we create a work environment that makes it more difficult to succeed. We can't build products the way we know we can. We can't support products the way we want to. We do a disservice to the customers, our colleagues, our products.

Resources don't build products. Resources can't think together. Resources don't create trusting relationships with each other and with customers.

People can do all of those things.

And, maybe, just maybe, we can think of the real resources in the organization. You know, the resources we buy with the capital equipment budget or expense budget, not the operating budget. The desks, the cables, the computers. Those resources. The ones we have to depreciate. Those are resources—not people.

We need all those resources such as desks, software, tool licenses, and all kinds of infrastructure to produce great software.

We also need people who can work collaboratively in teams.

These two things—physical resources and people—are different. Let's not forget that.

Resources are not people. People are not resources.

People become more valuable over time. Resources depreciate.

Consider that difference.

12.6 Options to Move From "Resources" to People

If I've intrigued you, here are some options to respect the people in your organization more:

1. Every time you hear the word, "resource," clarify: "Do you mean people?" Start with yourself first.

2. Does anyone feel the pressure to cut costs? If so, manage the project portfolio and see which projects/programs/products to cut. If you act early enough, you might discover you don't need to lay people off. You can choose which projects to cut and where to reassign people. (Read *Manage Your Project Portfolio: Increase Your Capacity and Finish More Projects, 2nd ed* [ROT16].)

3. Consider the culture you want to create and refine. Do you want to promote a mechanistic culture where you think the organization is a "well-oiled machine?" (It's not. It can't be. It never will be.) Or, do you want to consider a culture that optimizes *for* the humanness of the people in the organization? (I ask more questions in Book 3.)

CHAPTER 13

Do Experts Help Finish the Work?

Your organization might organize by function, such as UI people, front-end developers, back-end developers, testers, and more. At some point, the managers pick a bunch of people from the various functions, and say, "You, you, and you: you're a team now."

If the people learn how to work together and affiliate around the product, that team assignment can work.

However, if you recognize or reward people only based on their expertise, they will not work together. They will work separately. Worse, they won't share knowledge. Instead, they will reinforce the expertise each person has. You won't see a harmonic whole. You definitely won't see flow efficiency.

If you read Encourage Flow Efficiency on page 2, you might be willing to give me the benefit of the doubt. Maybe you'd like to see the delays as one team saw them before you make up your mind.

That's the point of this myth in organizations that only experts can perform a certain kind of work.

If you encourage experts and specialization, you will encounter significant delays.

13.1 Myth: Only 'The Expert' Can Perform This Work

Cliff, an IT Director, was concerned. One of the projects was a mess. It didn't seem to matter how much or how little the team had for requirements. The team never seemed to release enough on time.

Cliff had only been with the organization for four weeks. Yet, that team seemed to have more trouble than any of the other teams. He finally felt as if he had the trust of the VP and had figured out—at least a little—how to get things done here.

He'd just returned from meeting with Sandy, his VP. Sandy was frustrated and was ready for him to fire everyone and start with a new team. Cliff was pretty sure the team wasn't the problem. He needed to understand what the problem was and fast.

He decided to create a picture of how the team worked and where they had trouble. He asked the team members to gather in the meeting room at 3 P.M. that day.

"I need to understand what happens when you folks receive a project. I'm planning to graph the project timeline on the whiteboard, okay?"

One of the senior developers, Ellen, asked, "What are you going to do with this information?"

Cliff thought that was a strange question, but he answered. "I want to see where your time goes. Every time I walk by, I see you all busy at work. But, you seem to have trouble releasing."

Ellen nodded. So did everyone else.

"And then?" Ellen asked. "What will you do with this information?"

Cliff was puzzled. "What do you mean, do with the information?"

Ellen sighed. "Are you going to fire us?" she asked.

"No, that's not my intention at all," Cliff said. "If you're all working hard, why would I fire you?"

The team looked at each other. Teddy, the tester, said, "We've heard rumors . . ."

Cliff said, "Look, you know that I'm under pressure to 'make you perform better,'" he said. "I am not sure it's a function of your performance. I'm pretty sure we have a system problem. Let's see if we can understand what the system problem is."

Ted said, "I can tell you the system that's causing us problems. It's Deployment. We have to wait a week from the time we finish something until it's deployed. It doesn't matter how big this thing is, it's always a week."

Cliff went to the whiteboard. He put a sticky marked "T5" at the right end of the whiteboard. He wrote "Deployment" above the sticky.

"Thanks," Cliff said. "I was planning to start from the time we give you a project, but we could start from the release and work backward. What happens before you Deploy?"

Ellen said, "We have UAT. That takes two days."

Cliff asked, "For everything, regardless of the size?"

"Yup. It doesn't matter if it's something that took us two weeks or something that took us 30 minutes. First, we put in a request for UAT. That takes two days. Then they take 30 minutes to test and not with production data."

Cliff looked at her. "*Not* with production data?"

"Nope," she said. "We've given them access to our production data, but they won't use it. So, they don't really test what we developed."

Cliff said, "Wow, this is worse than I thought. You do have a system problem. You have several system problems." He wrote UAT on a sticky and labeled it T4. He put it to the left of the T5 sticky.

"Tell me more," he said.

The team graphed the rest of their project's process. It was worse than Cliff had expected. See Figure 13.1 on page 138.

The beginning of the process was okay. The VP and Cliff's peers decided which projects to do at T0. The team received the project at T1. Cliff wrote "Mgmt's decision time" between T0 and T1.

Then came a time that Cliff wasn't so sure about—the time between the time the project was put on the team's backlog and when the team started. Ellen had some data there. "Our previous product owner always had more we had to do on the previous project. That's one reason we started this project late."

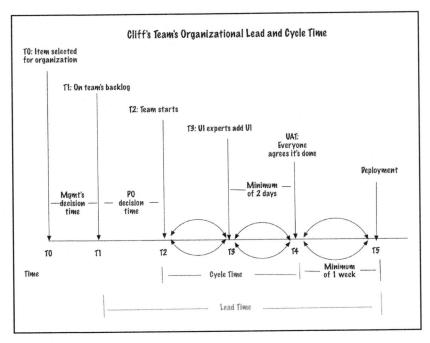

Figure 13.1: Cliff's Team's Interdependencies Due to Experts

Cliff said, "I'm not sure you started late if management and then your PO didn't tell you to start the project," he said. "That's what I mean by a system problem. If we want you to start a project, we should reduce—as much as possible—the time between T1 and T2." He paused. "How long was that time for this project?"

"Six months," Ellen said.

Cliff whistled. "That's a long time," he said.

"You bet," she said. "We started off behind."

"Okay," Cliff said. "I'll say 'PO decision time' there. Tell me more about the UI experts."

The team explained they weren't allowed to do any UI by themselves. They had to go to the UI group and ask for people. Because their project wasn't as important as other projects, they got new people all the time, who didn't understand their project.

The team iterated with the UI folks, which wasn't horrible, but it wasn't the same people all the time. They had to ask every time they needed a UI person.

Cliff looked aghast. "I'm sorry. I thought you folks were okay, just having deadline trouble. I didn't realize this was the problem. I should have paid more attention to you at the beginning."

Ellen smiled, more a wry grin. "You need all the political capital you have to deal with these problems," she said. "I'm not sure you could have taken this as your first quest."

Cliff smiled, "A quest, indeed! Okay, let's finish this. I assume that you find problems in the UI, and they find problems with your code?"

The team nodded.

"And, I bet it's the same thing with UAT and Deployment?"

The team nodded. Teddy said, "It's even worse. If UAT finds a problem, we always have to wait another two days. If Deployment finds a problem, we have to wait another week before they come around to us again."

"Have you measured your full cycle time?" Cliff asked.

Ellen said, "Yes, let me bring up our data for cycle time over the past three months, including UAT." She hooked her computer up to the projector and brought up the project's page. "Two months ago, our average cycle time was only four days. But something happened last month. I don't know what. Instead of UAT taking just two days, our request time jumped to four days. Our average cycle time is now eight days. And, don't get me started on Deployment."

Cliff asked, "Did you try to talk to anyone about this? I'm asking because I think there's something fishy here, and I want to know who I should talk with first and who I should talk with later."

They discussed who had helped the team in the past and who had been troublesome. Cliff took a picture of the whiteboard as a basis for discussion with Sandy.

Cliff made an appointment with Sandy for the next day. He brought his picture of the chart, cycle times, and lead times over the past three months. Once Sandy realized what was happening, he demanded a meeting with all of his directors to solve the problem.

It was time to relinquish the idea of working as experts.

13.2 Experts Cause Delays

The more experts you have inside the team and outside, the more delays a team encounters.

Many managers feel as if they have limited options when a project is waiting for The Expert. They can make the project wait, they can ask The Expert to multitask, or they can plug another expert into that job. After all, The Expert isn't needed full time on any one project, so it's okay, isn't it? Or, isn't any database administrator, senior tester, or release engineer just like any other, even if this one doesn't know your project backward and forward?

No, it's not okay at all. It's not okay to start a project starved of the people the project needs. It's not okay to ask a person to multitask. And, people who don't know your project aren't experts on *your* project.

There's another option. That option is to reduce the need for experts in several ways:

- Ask the experts to pair with others.
- Banish experts from your projects.
- Manage the project portfolio to stagger projects.
- Hire more experts.

My first choice is always to have the expert work with other people.

13.2.1 *Never Let Experts Work Alone*

Sometimes, an expert can duplicate his or her expertise. For example, maybe you only have one person who knows the build system, but everyone on a project needs to understand how to use the build system. In that case, I like to ask the one person who knows the build system to pair with each person on the team, one at a time, until every team member knows the build system as well as The Expert.

By never letting The Expert work alone, you have distributed the expertise among the team. Depending on the knowledge, you might need an internal workshop first so that everyone has the same baseline understanding of the tool or technology. Sometimes, it makes sense for the release engineer to conduct an internal workshop for a few hours to explain the inner workings of the build system and then pair with everyone to make sure each person understands how to use the system. You can use the same model for many of the activities of database administrators.

This approach works well for technical skill expertise that is primarily tool-based or based on a functional skill that is similar to another team member's functional skills. It doesn't work for everything. In cases where you have significant solution space domain expertise, where people need to know the guts of the code base, you want to consider other options, such as internal banishment.

13.2.2 Banish the Indispensable Expert

Some people appear to be indispensable. If they are working on another project and you want to touch "their code," your project must wait for them.

Don't fall for that nonsense. Banish those "indispensable" people from *your* project. Or, if they are working on your project, invite them to work on a different project. Whatever you do, move them off your project today.

If The Expert is inside your organization, but on another project, you still have access to The Expert. At some point, that expert will retire and start sailing the Caribbean sipping sweet rum drinks at 4 P.M., and you will not have access to The Expert. When do you want your team members to practice building their expertise? I want the team to practice while the expert is still available—but not holding the team hostage to their knowledge.

The team has unhealthy codependency on The Expert, and The Expert has a reciprocal dependency on the team. I'm no psychiatrist, nor do I play one on television, but in project terms, this is terrible. For the sake of The Expert's self-esteem, the entire team placates The Expert. This codependency has the effect of preventing the rest of the team from learning the product.

If you work in a large organization, as a manager, you can arrange for The Expert to transition to another project. In a small organization, you can arrange for The Expert to work on a particular project. Make sure that the project has plenty of deliverables, so The Expert is too busy to opine on the old project.

The team will learn how to learn together. Once you remove The Expert, the team has a shot at becoming a real team, because now team members share a common goal.

Once you remove The Expert, team members will work together, and fast, to discover what they don't know. They will share what they do know. But, you have to allow The Expert to be available for a limited time every week. Maybe one hour, and then only if the team is stuck. Encourage the team to develop and use tests instead of questions to discover how the product works.

13.2.3 *Stagger the Projects to Use The Expert*

Maybe you don't have an expert with a self-esteem problem. Perhaps you do have a limited number of experts with security expertise, and you need them full time on a project. And, maybe you expected Project A to be finished by now so Project B could start. But Project A is not yet done.

If Project A is more valuable than Project B, don't start Project B. If Project B is more valuable than Project A, stop Project A, and start Project B. Yes, it is that easy. (The discussions about relative project value are the difficult part.)

The hard part is the decision: which project is more valuable?

Project portfolio management is all about having difficult discussions at the organizational level, so you don't do two projects at the same time, slowing down both of them. When you manage the project portfolio, you optimize for the entire organization. You don't play zero-sum games internally so that no one succeeds.

Do the *minimum* work on the more valuable project. Release that project. Now, go to the other project.

For more information on how to manage your project portfolio, see *Manage Your Project Portfolio: Increase Your Capacity and Finish More Projects, 2nd ed* [ROT16]. I'll discuss the portfolio more in Book 3.

13.2.4 *Hire More Experts*

If you really want both Projects A and B to proceed simultaneously, you have to hire more people. Even so, it will take a while to hire more people and have them up to speed fast enough to make a difference. But hiring more people will help.

If you do hire more people, consider:

- Ask the teams to mob for a week or so when every new person starts. That way, nobody turns into an expert.
- Break the first team into two teams so each part of the original team can teach the new people what they need to know.
- Make sure each person works on one and only one project. Affiliate each person with a specific team (Project A *or* Project B) and don't move the people around.

Hiring more people is just one alternative. You might find the projects need to deliver less than everyone initially thought.

13.3 Understand the Root Cause

One of the reasons we have so much multitasking in our organizations is that we have so many experts with narrow expertise. The narrower the knowledge, the less any given project needs that person, but when you need that person, you *really* need that person.

We have many myths about needing Experts and Only Experts to perform specific work. There is some work that only experts can do. The real question is this: how much? I don't expect developers to become testers or vice versa. Nor do I expect UI designers to become security experts. But as a manager, I expect everyone on a project to learn enough about the project to be conversant about the entire project. And, most importantly, I expect experts to work with others to share their knowledge.

The more people you have who can take a more generalist approach to product development, the more flexibility you have for your projects. So when I say, "Work flows through a team," you agree with me and say, "Of course. How else would it work?"

As you reduce the need for The Experts, the teams raise everyone's technical competence and capability in your organization.

13.4 Options to Reduce the Dependence on Experts

Maybe you've only seen organizations with serial experts, where everyone works in resource efficiency. (To see the images of resource and flow efficiency, review Encourage Flow Efficiency on page 2.)

You might need to see your system of work first before you can address this problem:

- Create a picture of your team's flow of work as you saw in Figure 13.1: Cliff's Team's Interdependencies Due to Experts.
- Use the measurements in Visualize the System on page 158 to measure your team's cycle time and lead time.
- Consider calculating the cost of all the delays you have because you have experts who multitask between projects. You can

calculate the Cost of Delay due to the multitasking.[1] Or, read *Diving for Hidden Treasures: Uncovering the Cost of Delay in Your Project Portfolio* [RE14].

If I haven't convinced you that experts don't help the projects, see if these alternatives would help:

- Consider hiring more people, so the expert is not the only one with that expertise. For example, in Cliff's situation, the organization doesn't have enough UI to fully staff all the teams that need UI.
- Ask everyone to collaborate as a team, especially if they pair or mob. In Cliff's case, integrating the UAT people into the team would help the team test as they proceed.
- Ask the expert never to work alone. Again, in Cliff's case, asking the UI people to work with the team might help.

You might need a different alternative, especially if your organization has the same deployment problem as Cliff's does. Often, people create delays when they're trying to prevent problems. You have alternatives, and I'll discuss those in greater depth in Book 3.

---

[1] https://www.jrothman.com/mpd/portfolio-management/2014/02/cost-of-delay-multitasking-part-2/

CHAPTER 14

Who Do You Promote Into Management?

When I first moved into a management job, my boss said, "Congratulations, you're a manager!" Then, he told me to talk to HR about the forms I would need to fill out.

He didn't explain about one-on-ones, feedback, coaching, all the necessary activities of management. He didn't tell me I needed to collaborate with my peers to accomplish my management work. He definitely didn't explain interpersonal skills and influence to me!

I dutifully made an appointment with HR. They gave me the "Personnel Requisition Form." Yup, that was the form I needed to ask for an open requisition to hire someone. I asked about the hiring process. The person said, "Every manager does what he or she wants. We're there to support you."

I'd been a senior engineer last week. I was a manager now. I thought I knew what to do. I didn't. I wasn't a flaming disaster, but I wasn't very good at management.

Many newer managers echo my experience. I succeeded in my technical work. My manager noticed. I got that management promotion with no knowledge of or opportunity to practice my management skills.

No training. No mentoring. No feedback and offer of coaching. No practice. When we don't help new managers learn to manage themselves and lead others, we disrespect the management profession and the person who is new to management.

Inside of two years, I was back to being a senior technical contributor, a technical lead. And I wanted to be a manager!

A couple of jobs later, at a different company, my boss resigned. I wanted to take his role. I'd been managing projects successfully and thought I was now ready for people-management.

I was ready for the challenge of making the challenging *management* decisions. I saw how our lack of project portfolio decisions affected everyone. I saw how we didn't make wise client decisions and the costs of those decisions. We had difficult tradeoffs to make in the projects, and I was willing to make them. Those were management decisions. I was eager and ready to make those decisions.

I didn't get that management job. My boss's boss told me I wasn't ready because I didn't have sufficient interpersonal skills. He hired someone else.

Business decisions are one piece of management. I could not have *implemented* those decisions without the necessary interpersonal skills.

My new boss was amazing. She coached me to be the best manager I could be. She taught me about one-on-ones and how not to inflict help with my coaching for the people I served. She taught me about influencing across the organization. And, we focused on how I could delegate and how to draw my boundaries.

I learned a ton from her and appreciate her to this day.

Especially in technical fields, we don't consider the variety of skills managers need—especially the interpersonal skills. That means we don't think about the best person to promote into management and how to help that person acquire their necessary management skills.

Who is the best person to promote? It often is *not* the person with the best technical skills. You might still need some technical knowledge, and that depends on your role in the organization.

Once you're a manager, your interpersonal skills matter more than your technical skills. That's because managers work with and through other people.

If you're unsure of your interpersonal skills, you can learn them. They are skills, just like your technical skills.

If you always promote the best technical person, you deprive the team of someone who was performing great technical work. And, if that person does not want to do management work, you inflict a terrible manager on the team and deprive the team of a potentially great manager.

Too many technical managers think they must promote the best technical person to management. Not true.

14.1 Myth: I Must Promote the Best Technical Person to Be a Manager

"I need a little breathing room in my group," Carl said to Steve. "I have fifteen people reporting directly to me, and you and I both know that's way too many. I need to promote somebody, but I'm having a little trouble deciding who to promote." Carl shook his head as he looked at his org chart. "You're a director. You have plenty of experience promoting people, right? What should I do?"

"You should do what I do," said Steve. "Take the most talented technical person and make that person the manager. Then, you know you have the best person for the job."

Carl almost spat his coffee. "You're not serious, are you? You know what happened when we promoted Nancy a year ago. And that ended after a month. We had a revolt on our hands! All she can think about is databases. Little endians, big endians, cardinality, rows, joins—you name it. She was a disaster as a manager, and she didn't even want the management position. She wanted a promotion, but to be a principal or consulting engineer, not a manager."

Steve sighed. "What do we do?"

"We need a way to think about the kind of person the manager has to be and then think about who would fill that role," Carl said. "Remember, once we promote someone, we lose the technical work that the person performs. We need to make sure we get the management work. Maybe we should ask if anyone wants to be a manager."

"Who would want to be a manager?" Steve asked.

"Well, I like managing. I told you that I wanted to be a technical manager when you and I had our first one-on-one a while ago," Carl said.

"Oh, that's right. I forgot," Steve said.

Carl asked, "Do you like being a middle manager?"

Steve paused and said, "Well, I like setting the strategy, and I like making sure that our projects get done. I like making the project portfolio decisions, but sometimes I miss the technology. I wonder if I'm too far away from the technology now. I'm not a senior manager, and I'm not a first-line manager. I find middle management difficult sometimes."

"Well, you're honest," Carl said.

"That, I am. Okay, let's talk about your people more seriously. Do you need more of a catalyst—a cattle prod?" Steve asked and laughed.

"No. Nobody needs a cattle prod. We need to look at the qualities, preferences, and non-technical skills more. It's time to do a job analysis for the management position. Then, I think I'll ask the people in my group if anyone wants the job. I probably should have been grooming people as part of a succession plan all along. It's too late for that now, but I do know that we don't need the best technical person."

14.2 Management Skills Differ from Technical Skills

Managers perform different work than technical people do. They require different skills. Managers deliver distinct value to the organization because they facilitate the work other people do.

If you do a job analysis, you can see that there are two different career paths for technical people: technical and managerial. Do you want to reward a technical person with more money? That's great. That person might also need a technical promotion.

Do not automatically "reward" a technical person with a management promotion.

14.3 Differentiate Between Managers and Technical Leads

Sometimes, it's difficult to tell the difference between a first-line manager and a technical lead. There is no standard for what each person might do, and each organization is different. However, Figure 14.1 shows how I see the differences between technical and management work.

Management work		Interact with other managers to manage the project portfolio.
		Write the (dreaded) performance evaluation.
		Lead the hiring effort. Organize the hiring work.
		Assist the team with its ability to become a self-organizing team.
		Obtain hard resources for the team, such as lab space, capital equipment, desks, and chairs. (Depending on the type of team, assist with requirements clarification.)
		Offer feedback and coaching on interpersonal issues.
	Technical lead work	Offer feedback and coaching on technical issues (depending on the type of team).

Figure 14.1: Continuum of Technical Leadership and Management Work

Your technical lead position may be limited to providing coaching and feedback on only the technical issues. I don't mean that as a negative thing. For many technical leads, that's an enormous job. To do more would be overwhelming, especially if there are four or more people on the team.

And, some technical leads do more than that, operating much more in the management realm. Some technical leads do everything up to writing performance evaluations and managing the project portfolio. In my opinion, once they write evaluations and manage the project portfolio, they are managers.

If you look at the qualities, preferences, and non-technical skills required to perform the work, as well as the value that they provide daily, their overall value to the company is managerial, not technical.

14.4 What's the Value of the Work?

No matter what job you have or the role you are looking to fill, always ask yourself this question: What is the value of the work that the person will provide?

A long time ago, in a company far away, a colleague, Beryl, took a new job as the Director of Software Quality. She had a wide and varied group of people:

- Thirteen manual-only testers. Ten of them only had surface knowledge of the product.
- Two testers with automation knowledge and capability.
- Three performance engineers.

Beryl knew she couldn't manage the work of these eighteen people directly. She also knew she didn't need managers because all the people worked on the same product. She did need people who could help organize the work, and then coach and teach to raise everyone's level of capability.

Beryl's company wanted the product to work faster. And, they wanted to release the product more quickly.

The performance engineers excelled at discovering product speed problems. However, they couldn't both discover and fix those problems. The performance engineers needed to work across the organization with the product engineers.

The testers could not use mostly manual testing to help the company with faster releases. They had to use more automation, and everyone needed to learn how to automate. The testers would still have to do some manual testing, but the automation deficit was killing their release speed.

Beryl met one-on-one with each person to understand what they wanted from their careers. Several people wanted more in-depth technical capability. Some people wanted technical lead responsibilities.

Sam, one of the testers, was a very sharp guy who knew the code base inside and out. Beryl asked him to be a technical lead. He would lead the test automation effort. There were several pieces to that effort:

- Increase test automation of the regular tests, so the frequent releases wouldn't kill the testers and to provide faster feedback to the developers.
- Continually work with the testers to organize the tests.
- Understand how to coach the testers to be able to know where automation would work and where it wouldn't.

Beryl wanted to separate the technical leadership from the management, for now. Sam was happy to do that, and then as he said, "fade back to being a technical contributor." Sam's interest was in increasing everyone's capability, not in management.

Beryl explained two facts to HR: that this technical leadership role was important to the group's success and that Sam deserved more pay for these additional responsibilities. Beryl spent a few weeks discussing these facts with HR and finally was able to increase Sam's pay.

In those few weeks, Sam and the rest of the team had increased their automation. Also, the performance engineers saw what Sam did. The performance engineers adopted some of his ideas.

All the tests ran faster. Because the testers and performance engineers found and reported issues sooner, the developers started to fix them more quickly. The entire product became more stable. People no longer needed or wanted to work overtime to finish their work.

Technical leads fill vital roles that are not management roles in the organization. Technical leads and technical people tend to use their influence within the team, with their manager, and across technical teams. Sometimes, technical leads also influence other managers.

14.5 Managers Work Outside the Team

Managers expand their influence outside the team, as well as upwards and across the rest of the organization. While negotiation and influence skills may be necessary for both, what's important to technical people is not going to be as relevant to other managers.

Promoting a great technical person into a management position may handicap that person for influence and negotiation—unless that person has great empathy and rapport-building skills or wants to develop those skills. I don't know about you, but I didn't get into software because I had great empathy and rapport-building skills. I've worked to develop those skills over the years.

14.6 Great Technical People Can Be Great Managers

Don't get me wrong. Great technical people can be terrific managers if they want to be. I suggest asking people if they desire a management role before you promote them. Sometimes, when people want a promotion, they want a technical promotion, not a managerial promotion. Ask first.

Make sure you know the difference between a technical lead and a manager where you work. Know which role you want the person to fulfill. I addressed the problem of management time and how too many managers expect a first-level manager to be a player-coach in Book 1.

You may have heard that management is about controlling the activities and leadership sets the vision. That's wrong. And, that thinking is why we have managers who aren't leaders.

If we want managers who can lead, we need to offer new managers the chance to learn their management skills. And, to choose between management and technical work—at least, for now. (I'll address much more about leadership in Book 3.)

Your expectations of a technical lead might be different from mine. That's fine. Clarify the expectations for any role. Don't assume that the best person for the job is the best technical person.

14.7 Consider Your Promotion Options

Promoting someone into management is one of the most challenging decisions a manager makes. People rarely have all the necessary skills to make that transition. That's because they require practice for management skills. They can't get that practice until they start to work as a manager. It's a catch-22.

How can you tell who would make a good manager?

In an ideal world, you would meet one-on-one with the people you serve and ask them about their plans for their careers. If they say they would like management, you can help them if they want to acquire those management skills.

Consider these questions for the people you serve now:

- Who is the best person to promote? Do you need someone who already has sufficient technical and interpersonal skills, or can you take the time to train someone?
- Do you plan to be in your job forever? Even if you have no immediate plans to change jobs, every manager needs to practice succession planning.
- Do you know what every person you serve wants from their career, at least in the short-term?

Consider these questions for the management role(s) you need to fill:

- What kind of feedback and coaching skills does the role need?
- How much delegation will the candidate need to learn?
- How much influencing skills will this role require?

- What other management skills does the job require?

Let's consider how to prepare people for management roles and offer them a chance to practice.

CHAPTER 15

Where Will You Start Leading and Serving Others?

If you've read this far, you realize that managing other people means leading and serving them as a harmonic whole. Where will you start your journey?

Start with yourself.

No one told me or trained me to think about a harmonic whole. My managers wanted me to look at individuals and focus on the short term. Through practice and experience, I learned that flow efficiency works better than resource efficiency. I reconsidered my management practices. I hope you do, too.

How can you create a team or group that works as a harmonic whole? Consider these questions as you review your management practices:

- How can I, as the leader, help people collaborate with others, in a team, workgroup, or across the organization to finish work? How can I Encourage Flow Efficiency on page 2?
- How can I Create a Culture of Psychological Safety on page 6 so people can admit their mistakes and learn from them?
- How can I encourage people to use their autonomy, mastery, and purpose in service of our products and services? How can I Extend Trust on page 8 so people can do their best work?

As you review your behaviors, see where your leadership creates a culture of trust, respect, and accountability to and with each other.

If you're not sure where to start, consider ways to visualize your system. Remember, the environment—the system—affects everyone's behavior.

15.1 Visualize the System

You have several alternatives to visualize the system of work. Sometimes, you can draw a picture of what occurs with unexpected events and how the team manages those events:

- When people receive requests for additional or different tasks than they expected.
- When you or other people ask the people you serve to work on additional projects.
- When people felt they needed to help other teams.

I often discover a picture isn't enough, even if it looks like Figure 13.1: Cliff's Team's Interdependencies Due to Experts. I often discover I need to collect team-based measures that help the team see the effect of those events.

If you lead a software development team, consider the metrics in *Accelerate: Building and Scaling High Performing Technology Organizations* [FHK18]:

- Lead time, the total duration from the time a customer makes a request (customer might be a product person) until the time the team delivers the work that fulfills that request. Lead time includes all the time the senior management discusses the item, not just the time the team takes to deliver that work.
- Deployment frequency: How often a team deploys their completed work.
- Mean Time to Restore: If you have a problem in production, how long does it take to recover from that problem?
- Change fail rate: Deployment failures. How often does a deployment fail and you need to roll back?

These metrics require the team to attend to technical excellence. You can't go fast if you don't have supporting infrastructure, such as tests and the ability to deploy inside the team.

Depending on your role in the organization, you might be able to influence all four of these measures. However, every leader can ask the team to visualize their cycle time to see the bottlenecks and delays.

Cycle time is a team measure. And, it helps people see how the organization helps or prevents throughput.

15.1.1 *Help the Team Measure Their Cycle Time*

Cycle time is the entire time it takes a team to finish work, starting from the time the team takes the work until the team completes the work. Cycle time includes all the work times plus all the wait times.

The more you want to create a "harmonic whole," the more you need the team to collaborate on and complete smaller chunks of work.

In my experience, teams that measure their cycle time create a positive feedback loop. The more they measure cycle time, the more they tend to work in flow efficiency. And, the more they tend to work on smaller chunks of work, the more they work together. In turn, that lowers their cycle time.

When you Encourage Flow Efficiency on page 2, no one gets "credit" for their individual work, as in resource efficiency. Instead, the *team* receives all the credit for finishing the team's work.

I suggest you ask the team to measure their cycle time. You might need to facilitate the team's measurement of their cycle time if they don't know how to do so. You might use a generic value stream map to start. See Figure 15.1 on page 160.

Here's how to measure a team's cycle time: Look for the work time: the duration of time the item spends above the line. Add in the wait time, the length of time the item spends below the line.

How much of the team's time is in a work state? How much of the team's time is in a wait state?

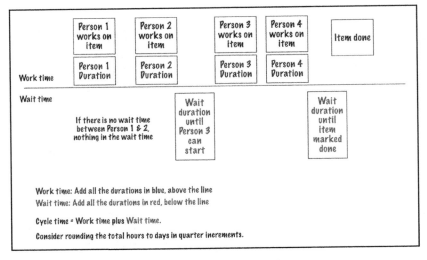

Figure 15.1: Generic Value Stream Map

Help the team create their value stream map for the last three or four features or whatever the team delivers:

1. Start with the very first state for the work item. That work starts above the line because the person doing the work adds value.

2. Now, count the time the item stays in that state with the same person. Keep the line in the value-add state, above the neutral line.

3. Once the first person transitions the work to the next person, decide if there is a delay or if that next person can work on the item right away. If there is a delay in adding value, show that delay below the neutral line. Once the next person adds value, we show the work above the neutral line.

4. Continue looping between numbers two and three until the team marks the work as done.

Make sure the team maps the flow they have, not the flow they want.

You might like the examples of cycle time in Measure Cycle Time, Not Velocity,[1] or *Create Your Successful Agile Project: Collaborate, Measure, Estimate, Deliver* [ROT17].

I do not recommend you measure the cycle time *for* the team. Their cycle time is their data. They need to learn how to measure cycle time themselves. And, it's possible that if you measure for the team, they will try to game the data.

Once the team has its cycle time data, ask them what they make of the data. You might ask these specific questions:

1. How much time does the team collaborate on a given work item? The more the team collaborates, the faster the team can proceed.
2. How much inside-the-team wait time does the team incur? When the team has internal wait time, they might not work in flow efficiency. And, they might have high WIP (Work in Progress).
3. How much does the team wait for external people? System problems almost always occur when the team waits for other people. If the people you serve have to wait for others— especially experts—you might need to solve that problem.

Look for reasons in the environment that the team might not work collaboratively:

- The team doesn't know how to pair, swarm, or mob.
- The team doesn't know how to offer or receive feedback or coaching, so the team isn't safe to collaborate.
- Someone else (possibly your manager) wants to *see* people working alone.
- The performance review system discourages collaboration and encourages individual work.
- The team has people who don't work well with others.

---

[1] https://www.jrothman.com/mpd/2019/09/measure-cycle-time-not-velocity/

These reasons are culture or environmental. In my experience, the environment prevents teams from collaboration.

The team you serve might have other reasons. Most teams can't solve these problems alone. They need someone to help remove impediments or arrange for training.

While cycle time is a team measure, lead time is an organizational measure of delays.

15.1.2 Measure Lead Time to See Organizational Delays

Lead time is all the time it takes the organization to ask a team to do work until the customers can use the work. This time includes decision-making time from the people who define the requirements, the team's cycle time, and whatever time it takes to release the team's work.

If you review Figure 13.1: Cliff's Team's Interdependencies Due to Experts, you can see that there are two additional delays before and after the team's cycle time. Those delays are the PO decision time, and the time it takes Deployment to release the product.

Cliff was able to work inside his department for the team's cycle time. However, he needed to work in the greater organization to reduce the lead time. I'll discuss this more in Book 3.

If you work with the team to determine all the delays: incoming work delays, and delays to the customer, you will discover many opportunities to serve the team.

15.2 Assess Your Current Behaviors

Consider your current behaviors and see if you want to experiment with them:

- In what ways do you help create a culture of psychological safety?
- In what ways do you extend trust, even before you think people have "earned" your trust?

- How do you help shape the environment so people can work as a harmonic whole?
- How do you live your value-based integrity?

The more you can work as a Theory Y manager, where you manage by exception, the easier your management will be, and the more productive the people you serve will be. You will set them free to do their best possible jobs.

15.3 Change Your Behaviors First

As an unseasoned manager, I saw too many jaded and cynical people. They kept their heads down. They did their work. They went home and did it again the next day.

I thought that was a dreary existence. My only goal was to see if I could create a little excitement or optimism about their work.

I started managing myself, primarily by not judging them. I continued with one-on-ones, feedback, and coaching. I added the idea of team-based work, team-based feedback, and coaching. I encouraged people to work in their own ways, and still work as a team.

I often had to be the team "protector." I had to shield my team from the craziness imposed by general management or HR. I had to create and refine the team culture so we could deliver what we needed to.

I wasn't always successful—especially when I bounced against management dictums. However, over the time I served these various people and teams, people became less jaded and cynical. They grew safe enough to collaborate. And, that safety outlasted my tenure as a manager. I'm thrilled with that.

15.4 You Don't Have to be Perfect

Remember the goal of managing others: to create an environment where people feel safe to collaborate so everyone wins: the customer, the organization, and the people.

As leaders, when we focus on how we serve others, we often achieve our goals obliquely.

Consider how you serve people now:

- Do you build sufficient relationships, so you know how people learn, work, and deliver?
- Can you focus on the team's throughput and outcomes, not an individual's output?
- Can you focus on the long term and not be entranced by quick fixes or silver bullets?

When you focus on the long term, work on your integrity and congruence, you are more likely to gain the results you want.

You don't have to be perfect at serving others. I have found it worthwhile to periodically examine my beliefs and actions to see if what I do helps or hurts my management.

I recommend you do the same.

15.5 Is Management For You?

After all this, you might wonder if management is for you. I like to think about the problems managers solve.

When you lead and serve others, you discover messy, systemic problems. You work with people to solve those messy problems.

As Weinberg said in *Secrets of Consulting* [WCO14],

"No matter how it looks at first, it's always a people problem."

Managers create a culture that creates—and can fix—those problems. You might make the best possible decisions at the time and still create problems in the future.

You might decide you don't want to solve culture or environment problems. If you are a manager now, consider when and how you can relinquish your management responsibilities. Don't torture yourself or the people you would serve by staying in a management role when that's not what you want to do.

15.6 **Our Journey**

You've read how to build respect, trust, and integrity in your relationships with each person and the team. That respect, trust, and integrity allows you to serve the people and the team.

In turn, those people respect and trust each other—and feel a sense of loyalty to you and the organization.

You've created an environment where people can do their best work.

If you just read this book, you might want to read Book 1. That's where you might consider your beliefs to build congruence and integrity in your actions.

Book 3 is about creating a human system in the organization, so you can use the ideas of respect, trust, and integrity to create a place people want to work.

Annotated Bibliography

[ADZ12] Adzic, Gojko. *Impact Mapping: Making a big impact with software products and projects*. Provoking Thoughts, 2012. Understand what you want to build.

[BAT15] Bateson, Nora. *Symmathesy: A Word in Progress*. At https://norabateson.wordpress.com/2015/11/03/symmathesy-a-word-in-progress/. Provocative ways to think about how people work and learn together. Includes ways to think about why you might not attempt a divide-and-conquer strategy for the people and the work.

[BUC99] Buckingham, Marcus and Curt Coffman. *First, Break All the Rules: What the World's Greatest Managers Do Differently*. Simon and Schuster, 1999. The first easily accessible book I read about the do's and don'ts of great managers.

[BUG19] Buckingham, Marcus and Ashley Goodall. *Nine Lies About Work*. Harvard Business Review Press. 2019. A wonderfully fresh perspective on what we've told ourselves about management and leadership—and have been wrong about for too long. }

[DEM13] Deming, W. Edwards. *The Essential Deming: Leadership Principles from the Father of Quality*. McGraw Hill. 2013. It's not a short book. And, I still recommend you read it. You might know Deming for his work in quality. The way he achieved successes was by teaching management.

[DOE18] Doerr, John. *Measure What Matters: How Google, Bono, and the Gates Foundation Rock the World with OKRs.* Penguin. 2018. The original text on OKRs, Objectives and Key Results. OKRs are not MBOs, Management by Objectives. Instead, OKRs talk about the outcomes the organization wants to achieve.

[DRU73] Drucker, Peter. *Management: Tasks, Responsibilities, Practices.* Harper Collins. 1973. Originally published in 1973 with reprints in 1985 and 1993, I consider this the bible of what modern management should be. If you're put off by his language, please read past his use of "man" as the only gender for manager. Us modern readers can substitute "people" for the word "man" and the content is as fresh and useful as it was back when Drucker first published the book.

[EDM12] Edmondson, Amy C. *Teaming: How Organizations Learn, Innovate, and Compete in the Knowledge Economy.* Jossey-Bass, San Francisco, 2012. How self-organized teams really work, and what we need to make them work in different cultures.

[FHK18] Forsgren, Nicole, Jez Humble, and Gene Kim. *Accelerate: Building and Scaling High Performing Technology Organizations.* IT Revolution, Portland OR. 2018. An eminently readable book about how to understand and measure software organizations.

[MOA13] Modig, Niklas and Pär Åhlström. *This is Lean: Resolving the Efficiency Paradox.* Rheologica Publishing, 2013. Possibly the best book about how managers should consider agile and lean. A wonderful discussion of resource efficiency vs. flow efficiency.

[MCG06] McGregor, Douglas. *The Human Side of Enterprise, annotated edition.* McGraw-Hill. 2006. Many managers think self-organization or self-managing teams are new with agile and lean approaches. McGregor originally published this book in 1960. At that time, he knew and encouraged managers, to trust the people the managers served.

[NOT10] Noteberg, Staffan. *Pomodoro Technique Illustrated: The Easy Way to Do More in Less Time.* Pragmatic Bookshelf. 2010. Wonderful introduction to a technique that helps you manage your work and finish it. Often, in less time than you imagined.

[PIN11] Pink, Dan. *Drive: The Surprising Truth About What Motivates Us.* Riverhead Books. 2011. All motivation is intrinsic: autonomy, mastery, and purpose. Once people believe they are paid fairly, it's all about autonomy, mastery, and purpose.

[PIN18] Pink, Dan. *When: The Scientific Secrets of Perfect Timing.* Riverhead Books, 2018. We each have times during the day when we excel at solving different kinds of problems: insight problems and analytical problems. And, we each have times when we cannot solve those the problem at hand. Sometimes, naps are the answer.

[BCD05] Rothman, Johanna and Esther Derby. *Behind Closed Doors: Secrets of Great Management.* Pragmatic Bookshelf, Dallas, TX and Raleigh, NC, 2005. We describe the Rule of Three and many other management approaches and techniques in here.

[ROT12] Rothman, Johanna. *Hiring Geeks That Fit.* Practical Ink, 2012. Learn to hire people, from writing a job description to a great first day. All the templates are available for free on Johanna's website. The book explains how to use them.

[ROT16] Rothman, Johanna. *Manage Your Project Portfolio: Increase Your Capacity and Finish More Projects, 2nd ed.* Pragmatic Bookshelf, Dallas, TX and Raleigh, NC, 2016. Sometimes, program managers encounter project portfolio decisions with the feature set, or the request for people to multitask. This book helps you manage all the work in your project portfolio. I also have more references about why multitasking is crazy in here.

[ROT17] Rothman, Johanna. *Create Your Successful Agile Project: Collaborate, Measure, Estimate, Deliver.* You don't need to adopt a specific framework for any given agile project. Instead, use the agile and lean principles to adjust for your project's context.

[RE14] Rothman, Johanna and Jutta Eckstein. *Diving for Hidden Treasures: Uncovering the Cost of Delay in Your Project Portfolio.* Practical Ink, 2014. A book about Cost of Delay and how to see how those costs affect your project portfolio.

[ROC08] Rock, David. "SCARF: A brain-based model for collaborating with and influencing others." NeuroLeadership Journal 1 (2008): 44–52.

[SSW97] Seashore, Charles, Edith Seashore, and Gerald M. Weinberg, *What Did You Say? The Art of Giving and Receiving Feedback.* Bingham House Books, 1997. If you haven't thought much about how to offer or receive feedback, this book is a gem. Even if you have considered how you might offer feedback, this book might change your mind about how you receive and act on feedback.

[SCO17] Scott, Kim, *Radical Candor: Be a Kick-Ass Boss Without Losing Your Humanity.* St. Martin's Press, New York, 2017. If you want to see plenty of feedback traps and tips, this is a terrific book.

[SCH10] Schein, Edgar H. *Organizational Culture and Leadership.* Jossey-Bass. San Francisco 2010. Culture is not about the color of the walls or the foosball tables. Culture is about us, as humans. A fascinating look at what culture means.

[SOF01] Solomon, Robert C. and Fernando Flores. *Building Trust in Business, Politics, Relationships, and Life.* Oxford Press, 2001. This book helped me see that extending trust is often the basis of creating great relationships. The parts about integrity are also useful for anyone, not just managers.

[WCO14] Weinberg, Gerald M. *The Secrets of Consulting: A Guide to Giving and Getting Advice Successfully.* 2014. An excellent book for understanding what consulting is—and is not. Full of rules and aphorisms, you will learn what to do as a consultant, and as a manager. Cheap and fun learning.

[WEI93] Weinberg, Gerald M. *Software Quality Management, Vol 2: First-Order Measurement.* Dorset House Publishing, New York, 1993. This particular Weinberg book has excellent definitions of congruence and human interaction.

[WOD16] Wodtke, Christina. *Radical Focus: Achieving Your Most Important Goals with Objectives and Key Results.* 2016. A business fable that clearly explains OKRs.

[WOO10] Woolley, Anita Williams, Christopher F. Chabris, Alexander Pentland, Nada Hashmi, and Thomas W. Malone. *Evidence for a Collective Intelligence Factor in the Performance of Human Groups.* Science, September 30, 2010 DOI: 10.1126/ science.1193147. Also online at https://www.sciencedaily.com/ releases/2010/09/100930143339.htm

Specific references for why performance reviews don't work:

- *First, Break All the Rules: What the World's Greatest Managers Do Differently* BUC99.
- *Nine Lies About Work* BUG19.
- Hope, Jeremy and Robin Fraser, *Beyond Budgeting: How Managers Can Break Free from the Annual Performance Trap* (Boston: Harvard Business Press, 2003).
- Kohn, Alfie, *Punished by Rewards* (New York: Houghton-Mifflin, 1993).
- Pfeffer, Jeffrey, *The Human Equation: Building Profits by Putting People First* (Boston: Harvard Business School Press, 1998).
- Pfeffer, Jeffrey, *What Were They Thinking? Unconventional Wisdom About Management* (Boston: Harvard Business School Press, 2007).

- Pfeffer, Jeffrey and Robert I. Sutton, *Hard Facts, Dangerous Half-Truths And Total Nonsense: Profiting From Evidence-based Management* (Boston: Harvard Business School Press, 2006).
- Hope, Jeremy, and Steve Player *Beyond Performance Management: Why, When and How to Use 40 Tools and Best Practices for Superior Business Performance* (Boston: Harvard Business Review Press, 2012).
- Chandler, Tamra M., *How Performance Management is Killing Performance—and What to Do About It* (Oakland: Berrett-Koehler Publishers, 2016).
- Austin, Robert D., *Measuring and Managing Performance in Organizations* (New York, Dorset House Publishing, 1996).

More from Johanna

I consult, speak, and train about all aspects of managing product development. I provide frank advice for your tough problems—often with a little humor.

If you liked this book, you might also like the other books I've written: https://www.jrothman.com/books/:

Practical Ways to Manage Yourself: Modern Management Made Easy, Book 1

Practical Ways to Lead and Serve—Manage—Others: Modern Management Made Easy, Book 2

Practical Ways to Lead an Innovative Organization: Modern Management Made Easy, Book 3

Write a Conference Proposal the Conference Wants and Accepts

From Chaos to Successful Distributed Agile Teams: Collaborate to Deliver

Create Your Successful Agile Project: Collaborate, Measure, Estimate, Deliver

Manage Your Project Portfolio: Increase Your Capacity and Finish More Projects, 2nd ed

Agile and Lean Program Management: Scaling Collaboration Across the Organization

Diving for Hidden Treasures: Uncovering the Cost of Delay Your Project Portfolio

Predicting the Unpredictable: Pragmatic Approaches to Estimating Project Cost or Schedule

Project Portfolio Tips: Twelve Ideas for Focusing on the Work You Need to Start & Finish

Manage Your Job Search

Hiring Geeks That Fit

Manage It!: Your Guide to Modern, Pragmatic Project Management

Behind Closed Doors: Secrets of Great Management

In addition, I have essays in:

Readings for Problem-Solving Leadership

Center Enter Turn Sustain: Essays on Change Artistry

I'd like to stay in touch with you. If you don't already subscribe, please sign up for my email newsletter, the Pragmatic Manager, on my website https://www.jrothman.com. Please do invite me to connect with you on LinkedIn, or follow me on Twitter, @johannarothman.

I would love to know what you think of this book. If you write a review of it somewhere, please let me know. Thanks!

—Johanna

Index

Printed in Great Britain
by Amazon